Power Pack Your Job Search!

Anne Follis is an outplacement specialist, a certified professional résumé writer (CPRW), and the owner and manager of Career*Pro* in Peoria, Illinois. She prepares original résumés and business proposals, conducts outplacement seminars, and counsels individuals at all levels on career decisions. She brings a background of author, educator, lecturer, administrator, and home-maker to her job of helping others in their quest for employment.

Power Pack Your Job Search!

Anne Follis

Baker Books

A Division of Baker Book House Co
Grand Rapids, Michigan 49516

© 1997 by Anne Follis

Published by Baker Books
a division of Baker Book House Company
P.O. Box 6287, Grand Rapids, MI 49516-6287

Printed in the United States of America

All rights reserved. No part of this publication may be reproduced, stored
in a retrieval system, or transmitted in any form or by any means—for
example, electronic, photocopy, recording—without the prior written permission of the publisher. The only exception is brief quotations in printed
reviews.

Library of Congress Cataloging-in-Publication Data

Follis, Anne Bowen, 1947–
    Power pack your job search! / Anne Follis.
        p. cm.
    Includes bibliographical references.
    ISBN 0-8010-5730-2
    1. Job hunting—United States. 2. Job hunting—Religious
aspects—Christianity. I. Title.
HF5382.75.U6F65 1997
650.14—dc20   96-8735

Unless otherwise indicated, Scripture quotations are from the HOLY
BIBLE, NEW INTERNATIONAL VERSION®. NIV®. Copyright © 1973,
1978, 1984 by International Bible Society. Used by permission of Zon-
dervan Publishing House. All rights reserved.

Scripture quotations identified GNB are from the *Good News Bible*—Old
Testament: Copyright © American Bible Society 1976; New Testament:
Copyright © American Bible Society 1966, 1971, 1976.

To Dean,
my rock

And to Jesus Christ,
our Rock

Contents

Introduction   9

1 Here We Go Again   13
   Updating Your Job Search Strategy
2 Just Who Are You?   18
   Preparing Your Inventory
3 A Portrait in Words   26
   Writing an Effective Résumé and Cover Letter
4 The Search Is On   42
   Generating Leads
5 "May I Have a Moment of Your Time?"   48
   Telemarketing Your Way to Success
6 Whatsoever Things Are Good   54
   Keeping Your Eye on the Prize
7 Employment Agencies and Headhunters   59
   Finding Your Way through the Jungle
8 Don't Get Caught without Backup   63
   Supplying References
9 Are You Worth Your Weight in Gold?   67
   Responding to Salary Questions
10 You're On!   72
   Succeeding at the Interview
11 "Some of My Best Friends . . ."   85
   Dealing with Discrimination

Contents

12 "So, You're a Christian . . ."   90
   Facing Religious Discrimination
13 Don't Go with the Flow   99
   Making a Difference
14 Slings and Arrows   104
   Surviving the Tough Times
15 Recession-Proof Your Job Skills   111
   Planning for the Future
16 Depression-Proof Your Spirit   116
   Looking to the Future

   Appendix: How to Choose a Résumé Service   118
   Notes   124
   Recommended Reading   125

Introduction

She was bright and well educated, and she had excellent credentials; nevertheless, her job had been eliminated.

"After fifteen years," she moaned as she sat in my office poring over her work history. "And my husband left me six months ago. So . . ." (she rolled her eyes) "for the first time in fifteen years I'm looking for a job *and* I'm dating." There was a long pause. Finally she said definitively, "They've both changed a *lot*."

I can't speak to the dating situation, but I, like most people who have been through the job search process, would agree that if anything her comment about job hunting is an understatement.

According to job-change guru Richard Nelson Bolles,

> We are experiencing a *Workquake*
> Just like an earthquake
> Something of the magnitude that shook San Francisco back in '89
> When part of the Bay Bridge fell, and buildings we had counted on
> Suddenly became unsafe.[1]

We are indeed experiencing a "workquake," which I see evidence of every day in my job as a résumé writer and outplacement consultant. Downsizing, also called "workforce reduction," "negotiated departure," "restaffing," and a host of other euphemisms, is the trend as companies rebound from a decade or more of overspending and adapt to an increasingly global economy. "Firings used to be done with surgical cleanliness," writes Harvey Mackay in his best-seller, *Sharkproof.* "Now they're called restructurings, and they're done with a meat cleaver."[2]

The reality of the '90s is that the number of higher paying manufacturing jobs is down, the number of lower paying service jobs is up, companies are cutting back, household incomes are declining, and there's a significant increase in part-time and temporary positions. In fact, some companies are hiring what are called "permanent temporaries" (an ingenious term): permanent employees who have temporary status, and therefore, lack job security or benefits. And nobody is immune anymore; white-collar workers have been hit as hard as blue-collar workers. The old sense of stability is gone. In this brave new world, a worker can expect to change jobs eight to ten times in a lifetime, and to change careers three or more times.

This means it's time to fasten your seat belt because somewhere along the line you're likely to find yourself caught up in the whirlwind of hitting the want ads and pounding the pavement looking for employment. And when that happens, one of the first things you'll find is that there are a whole lot of people out there doing exactly the same thing. The competition is fierce—it's clearly a "buyer's market"—and you are sure to face plenty of rejection.

Back in the olden days, say, around 1975, if you were unemployed or looking to change jobs, you answered ads in the papers and filled out applications, and then you waited for the phone to ring. Today if that's all you do, you're likely to have a long wait. It's essential to develop an up-to-date strategy for finding what you're looking for because, as my client so wryly observed, the whole process has changed a *lot*. *You* must take responsibility for your own job search. You must analyze your skills, figure out how to present them effectively both over the phone and on paper, find companies for which you might like to work, learn about those companies, ferret out the people within those companies who do the hiring and develop a strategy for approaching them, and follow up on any and all contacts. You will have to approach this as a job and invest a given amount of time per day to this effort. You must organize your list of contacts and keep careful records of whom you spoke to and when and what they said. You must brace yourself for rejection—quite possibly a whole lot of it—and approach every no as just one more on the way to the right yes. This book will take you step by step through each of these aspects of the job search process.

But, of course, dealing with the uncertainty of unemployment (or *under*employment, another result of our downsizing times) involves more than mapping out a clever strategy. Losing a job can be one of the most traumatic life events, right up there with death and divorce. I have a box of tissues sitting next to my desk, and I've had more than one grown man, and woman, sit in my office and cry. Career transition is often accompanied by a deep sense of betrayal and injustice. I played by the rules, I worked hard, and I had an understanding with God: This wasn't going to happen to me. Rejection, a sure companion to every job seeker, can be devastating to ego and morale, and mounting bills can test faith to the limit. How are we as God's people to hold our ground as the "workplates" beneath our feet give way?

One white-collar executive described his experience this way: "My foundation turned out to be sand." But this business of foundations is just what Jesus talked about in the parable of the wise man who built his house on a rock, and the foolish man who built his house on the sand (Matt. 7:24–27). Contrary to popular opinion, the foundation for our lives isn't job security, good benefits, a generous retirement package, and a regular paycheck, much as we may have come to depend on these things. And so, even as you mount a well-oiled campaign to land a job, it's important to remember just who is in control and where the true source of your security lies.

This book is written with the hope of providing a balance of practical advice and spiritual encouragement for the growing number of people who are, as they say, in the job market. So if you just got fired and don't know where to begin, read on. If you've been looking for months and want to give up, read on. If you're working twice as hard for half the money and want to know how to get off the merry-go-round, read on. And if you're beginning to wonder if God has forgotten you, read on.

It is my earnest prayer that this book will help you stay on track as you maneuver a career transition, and that through this experience you will set your roots deeper in Christ, build your life on him, and become ever stronger in your faith (Col. 2:7). Many people have walked through this valley and have come out stronger and wiser, and no worse for wear. You can too.

I'm sure of it.

1

Here We Go Again

Updating Your Job Search Strategy

If you're like most job seekers, you invest the majority of your time and precious resources in responding to ads in the newspapers. That, after all, is the way our grandparents went about finding employment, and if it was good enough for them . . .

Reality check. Estimates vary, but if that's the strategy you're using to find a job, indications are that your likelihood of success is around 10 to 13 percent. No wonder people get depressed and quit before they find a job. It can be like pounding your head against a brick wall.

The problem is that there are a lot more people looking for jobs these days than there are jobs available. (I'll bet you already figured that one out!) Consequently, when an ad hits the newspaper, it's not uncommon for an employer to receive hundreds of responses, if not thousands. One major manufacturer in central Illinois ran an ad for factory workers and received more than seventeen thousand résumés within just a few weeks.

Seventeen *thousand* résumés. Can you imagine opening, much less reading, seventeen thousand résumés?

That's an extreme example, but it's an indication of the kind of response one newspaper ad can generate. In addition, it's not unheard of for employers to run ads just to get a feel for the kind of talent that's out there without any immediate plans to do any hiring. I've even heard of employers running ads just to scare their own workers. Also, many companies run employment ads and then turn around and hire from within.

So if your primary strategy for finding a job is to answer ads in the newspaper, you are in reality responding to a number of ads that are, for all practical purposes, not legitimate. For the many other ads that are genuine, you are competing with up to thousands of other applicants, making the odds against you pretty overwhelming. No wonder you've begun to feel as if you're dropping your résumé into a black hole! There's got to be a better way.

There is, but it's going to take some hard work and initiative on your part. If you enjoy sales and marketing, it will be right up your alley, because for this little window of time (i.e., while you are trying to find a job) you are in sales, and the product you're marketing is you. And in case you haven't figured it out yet, there are lots of other "products" out there. Some of them are cheaper, some of them are smarter, some of them are older, some of them are younger, some of them have more experience, and some of them have less. It would be nice to think that the most qualified applicant will be the one who lands the job, but it frequently does not work that way.

Put yourself in the position of the person doing the hiring. You have an opening you have to fill within two weeks. You have two hundred résumés on your desk and counting. You would love to shut down the office

"DEAR MOM AND DAD . . . REACHING HIGH PLACES IN MY NEW JOB, AND THANKS FOR THE LOVELY DESK SET YOU SENT ME. . . ."

for the next fourteen days until you've settled this matter, but that's not at all practical. And so you get the awful job of sifting through résumés and calling people to come in for interviews while still performing all the other functions of your position, and you would rather submit to a root canal without an anesthetic.

And then some eager beaver (let's call him Joe) gets a hold of you on the phone. Actually, he's been calling for weeks. He's talked to your secretary and sent you letters and dropped off his résumé and then dropped off another copy "just in case the first one was lost." Finally, he calls early one morning before your secretary gets in, just as you are facing the prospect of going through all those résumés. He is pleasant and polite and to the point. He tells you briefly what his skills are, he expresses an interest in your company, and he asks about employment openings.

15

On the one hand, this call is a little annoying. On the other hand, you look at the growing stack of résumés and think, "This guy seems to know a little something about what we do around here, and he's awfully eager." And at a subconscious level you're even thinking, "If he works out, I won't have to go through all these résumés." He presses a little bit. "Would it be possible for me to come in and speak with you? I promise I won't take up too much of your time, but I would appreciate just a few minutes to introduce myself and present my qualifications in person. Would today be okay or would sometime later in the week be better?"

What would you say? If you're like the hundreds of managers I've talked to who have been through this, you're likely to say, "I've got a little time this afternoon if you can be here at 3:00." So Joe gets a crack at the job, while the two hundred applicants who simply sent in résumés and then sat around twiddling their thumbs hoping for the phone to ring may very well be history.

What made Joe stand out? Is he smarter or more qualified? Not necessarily. He was simply the one who called the right person at the right time.

But, you say, how can you possibly know when to call whom?

You can't. And so what you do is make a volume of phone calls (I recommend ten to twenty or more a day) and persist through a thousand stalls, rejections, and maybes until you touch base with the right person at the right time who says yes. It's that simple. And that difficult.

Before you moan and groan and say that you can't do it, that it's not your style, let me reiterate. In the past, the approach to getting jobs was passive. You sent out résumés and waited, hoping for a response. Since back in the good old days there were more jobs than people to fill them, you usually didn't have to wait very long, and this approach worked most of the time.

But we've already established that the world has changed—a *lot*—and today the onus is on the job seeker. You must take an active, persistent, aggressive approach to finding the job you want. If you don't do it, no one will. That I can guarantee. And my experience has been that for many people the process can be exciting and empowering. Rather than submitting helplessly to the whims of the job market, which can be the most depressing experience of a lifetime, you are taking control of the process for yourself.

Before you begin, you need to map out a strategy. First, you need to assess your skills and accomplishments.

There's a method to the madness of looking for a job, there really is, and it can be used effectively by everyone from an entry-level factory worker to an upper-level executive.

And it's time to get started!

2

Just Who Are You?

Preparing Your Inventory

I need a résumé," began the caller. "How much do you charge?"

"Well," I replied, "it depends on a lot of factors. Can you tell me a little bit about the kind of job you're looking for?"

"I just want a good job with benefits."

"Can you tell me something of your employment background? How many years of experience do you have?"

"I've been working since I was sixteen."

"At what kind of jobs?"

"Oh, I've done everything."

I could go on, but you get the picture. This conversation, or a variation of it, repeats itself with some regularity, and I am continually amazed at the number of people who cannot provide concrete answers to even the simplest of questions regarding their work objective or experience. When I press, or when they come in for an appointment, I discover they are secretaries, mechanics, electricians, retail managers, or accountants, with a variety of skills and accomplishments. But I think it's safe to say that if they can't tell *me* what they want to do or what they've done, they aren't going to express themselves with much clarity to a prospective *employer* either. It's easy to perform a job forty or more hours a week and take for granted all that the job entails. As a matter of fact, *most* people lack a clear understanding of just what they do for a living. An engineer says, "What do you mean *what do I do?* I design things." An office manager says, "Uh, well, I supervise people and work at the computer." A machine operator says, "You know, I run machines."

Regardless of where you're coming from, if you're going to sell yourself to an employer and be noticed above the crowd, it's essential that you size up what you've done and what you can do by conducting a personal inventory. So get out a pad of paper; we're going to be doing a little brainstorming.

Before we get to specific accomplishments, it's important to get a clear fix on the skills you have to offer, and these are divided into "hard" and "soft."

"Hard skills" are those that you can test and measure. They might include:

- type fifty words per minute
- know WordPerfect 6.0 and Lotus 1–2–3
- have a thorough understanding of accounting procedures, including accounts payable and receivable, taxes, payroll, and general ledger
- operate a lathe and drill press
- operate a forklift
- have mastered the skills involved in shipping and receiving

- experienced in mechanical engineering
- experienced in public speaking
- have achieved success in business writing

Think hard about every job you've ever done, volunteer or paid, and write down all the skills you have developed and proven. While brainstorming, nothing is off-limits, no matter how trivial or remote. Any idea may spark another idea, so keep writing. Take some time with this and enlist the help of someone who knows you well. It's difficult to be objective about yourself, but if you work with another person, you'll be surprised at what you'll come up with.

Next come the "soft skills." These are not as concrete, and they tend to be subjective. This is where you look inside yourself and think about the kind of person you are, what you like to do, and what you're good at. A list of soft skills might include:

- interpersonal communication
- analytical thinking
- work well under pressure
- able to manage a variety of jobs at the same time
- work well with children
- enjoy working with older people
- mechanical aptitude
- good phone skills
- good at negotiation
- persistent
- like to work alone
- like to work on a team
- organizational skills
- eye for detail
- relate well to the public

Again, do a mental check of all the jobs you've done, think about how you like to spend your free time, and work with a friend in developing as long a list as you possibly can.

If you're a new graduate or a homemaker who hasn't worked outside the home for a number of years, or if your experience is limited, it's likely your soft skills list will exceed your hard skills list. Lots of people tell me they have no experience, but that's almost never the case, so don't allow yourself to think in those terms. Your accomplishments may relate more to volunteer positions; for example, elected class treasurer, reorganized record-keeping procedures, tutored disadvantaged children for a local shelter, supervised a fundraiser for the Junior League that was the most successful ever. These are valuable accomplishments, and they tell a prospective employer important things about your capabilities.

Have you got writer's cramp yet? That's the idea!

Now let's do accomplishments.

It's common for clients to look at me with a blank stare or even to squirm uncomfortably when I ask them about accomplishments. Most people don't think they have any, but most of them are wrong.

Employers, whether consciously or unconsciously, tend to lump employees into two categories: people who are part of the problem and people who are part of the solution. Accomplishments are those things you've done that make you part of the solution. They're things that make work flow faster, that save money, or that result in greater harmony among workers.

Your list of accomplishments might include:

- streamlining office procedures
- writing a procedures manual

- figuring out how to make a machine operate more efficiently
- fixing a machine that broke down
- bringing a project in under budget
- continually completing work under deadline
- progressing in responsibility
- resolving a conflict
- reducing turnover
- implementing a training program
- scouting suppliers to save money on the purchase of materials or equipment
- adapting computer software to a specific project
- getting your department on-line
- developing a positive relationship with customers
- having a good work record of steady employment, punctuality, and little or no sick days

Brainstorm, brainstorm, brainstorm! You have brought a measure of creativity and originality to every job you've ever done, and this exercise is of critical importance. Unless you have a clear picture of what you have to offer, you will not be able to present yourself effectively to the person on the other side of the desk.

Now go back over your lists and narrow them down. I recommend writing them into three paragraphs. Even if you hate to write, and a lot of people do, the process of putting your hard skills, soft skills, and specific accomplishments into paragraph form will force you to put them into words that you can use when talking to a prospective employer. More important, it will also help you narrow down your job objective, which will be helpful when putting together a résumé.

If you're lucky, you have a clear, specific objective in mind: executive secretary, cost accountant, manufacturing quality control supervisor, operations manager, electrical engineer. But for a growing number of people, finding a neat, definite career objective is difficult. The problem is that they've held different jobs, they have a range of skills, and they aren't quite sure what they're looking for. In addition, few people these days want to limit their options. A retail manager might be interested in sales; a secretary might be willing to consider a customer service assignment; a blue-collar worker might be open to a position as a machine operator, an assembly worker, or a mechanic; a law enforcement officer might be interested in insurance claims investigation.

As you review your lists, cross off or pare down things that don't interest you. Perhaps you have a background in accounting and customer service. You love the number crunching and you're a whiz with figures, but you find the endless problem solving with customers distracting and boring. If that's the case, tone down (or eliminate) the emphasis on customer service and instead stress your accounting expertise, both on your résumé and when speaking to a hiring manager.

Or you might have held several jobs and developed a variety of skills that complement one another but don't necessarily add up to a clear objective. Let's say you worked for a while as a personnel assistant, then you took a job as a manager for a busy retail outlet, and more recently you worked for several years in customer service, providing assistance to a corporate clientele. When going over your experience, you might lay it out this way:

As a personnel assistant you gained computer and general office experience, as well as a knowledge of human resource procedures and benefit administration (hard skills).

As a retail manager you gained experience in personnel supervision, merchandising, and customer service (hard skills), as well as problem solving, working under pressure, and effectively balancing a demanding load of diverse responsibilities (soft skills).

As a customer service representative you fine-tuned your interpersonal skills in relating to different personalities (soft), and you demonstrated the ability to listen, make good judgments, and remain cool under stress (soft). In addition, you gained a keen understanding of the procedures of various corporations in your dealings with their representatives. You know, for example, the requirements of just-in-time inventory management in manufacturing and effective merchandising in retail. These count as hard skills, as there are positions where an understanding of these things would be of the utmost importance.

Now pull it all together. You are open to a number of opportunities, so you don't want to limit yourself, but there are some things you don't want to do. You may enjoy an office and business environment but have no interest in getting back into retail. At the same time, you'd be good in an office management position, but the only time you had management and supervisory experience was in retail. If that's the case, you'll want to stress the hard and soft skills you gained in your other positions, mention your supervisory experience, and tailor your retail experience to complement your other abilities.

You might tell an interviewer: "I have fourteen years experience in multiple organizational settings, including ten years office experience, and throughout my career I have thrived in a fast-paced environment. I have a good knowledge of computer operations and general office procedures, I offer supervisory and general management experience, and I have excellent communication and problem-solving skills in relating to people at all levels."

That sounds good, but can you make yourself stand out from all the other people who have similar experience by noting some of your accomplishments? To do so, you might say something like the following: "Of particular interest is my ability to streamline procedures to improve overall efficiency. For example, in my last position I reorganized the filing system and worked with a programmer to put it on the computer. As a result, when customers called we were able to pull their records in less than half the time."

With the hard skills, soft skills, and accomplishments pulled together from the above scenario, you'd be able to apply for a position as an office manager, administrative assistant, secretary, customer service supervisor, or any number of other possibilities.

Now that you're armed with a keen sense of what you have to offer, you'll need to put together a powerful résumé, develop a list of companies where you may want to work, begin networking with friends and acquaintances, make contacts, follow up, and track everything that you do. You don't have to be particularly clever or talented to be effective at this, just polite and persistent. Keep reading!

3
A Portrait in Words

Writing an Effective Résumé and Cover Letter

A résumé is a list of your jobs and education, right? Yes, of course, but it's a great deal more than that. When you send out a résumé, it's likely to land in a pile with dozens, maybe hundreds, of other résumés. When people screen résumés, they do so very quickly and with the goal of getting rid of as many as possible. It's a negative screening process. In other words, most people who look at your résumé on first glance are looking for an excuse to throw it away. An initial screening is usually very short, somewhere between seven and thirty seconds . . . if you're lucky. Your goal in preparing a résumé is to get past that first screening so you can get in the door for an interview. To do so, your résumé will have to be more than a list of jobs; it will have to be a carefully crafted marketing tool that you can use to sell yourself in a highly competitive market.

When writing a résumé, there are certain hard and fast rules that apply under all circumstances. A résumé must be:

- neat
- professional in appearance
- concise
- easy to follow
- well written
- free from grammatical and spelling errors
- written in the first person
- targeted toward what you can do for an employer

It also doesn't hurt to make your résumé a little bit distinctive. Most important, however, never lie on your résumé, no matter how tempting. As with all marketing tools, you can choose the emphasis of the résumé and you need not tell everything, but an outright lie will undermine your character and reputation and is sure to come back to haunt you.

"I MUST ADMIT, MR. FARNSLEY, I THOUGHT I HAD SEEN JUST ABOUT EVERY TYPE OF 'ATTENTION GRABBING' RESUME OUT THERE, BUT . . ."

A few less dogmatic principles also apply, though good résumé writers occasionally make exceptions to them.

Since we read from left to right, a résumé that is written in a left to right style, rather than one that is centered, is easier to follow.

Use action verbs to begin descriptive phrases. For example, the phrase "*Responsible for* personnel supervision, customer relations, and account maintenance" becomes much more powerful when it reads "Directly *supervise* a support staff of twelve, *maintain* positive customer relations, and *oversee* the maintenance of key accounts."

Even though your résumé is written in the first person, avoid the use of personal pronouns. Note in the example above the personal pronouns ("*I* directly supervise . . ., *I* maintain . . ., *I* oversee . . .") are understood. Omitting them gives the document an objective and professional tone.

While it is important to follow certain accepted principles when writing a résumé, it is just as important to avoid following common myths.

"A résumé should sound stuffy and pretentious." Wrong! It should sound professional, but to some degree it should reflect who you are. After all, it's your résumé! Avoid the use of big words when smaller ones will do. For example, deep-six "familiarity with" when you can say "familiar with" (Have you ever heard anyone use the phrase "familiarity with" in a sentence?), or "utilize" when you can say "use," or "interface" when you can say "communicate." And whatever you do, don't fall into the trap of using the third person by putting

an *s* on the end of verbs when writing job descriptions, as in "[she] manages all operations, [she] supervises staff," and so on. The résumé has your name, address, and phone number at the top, and it's usually accompanied by a personal cover letter. It is artificial, to say the least, to write it as if it's from someone else.

"A résumé should be no longer than one page." Not necessarily. Writing a résumé is something of a balancing act. People who read résumés are usually very busy and don't want any more information than they need, but if you have diverse experience that is important to the job you're applying for, then you may be better off going to two pages rather than selling yourself short. Two pages are usually the max, however, unless you're a doctor or a college professor with umpteen publications and years of experience to your credit.

"You have to put everything in your work and educational history on a résumé." Hardly. *Résumé* is a French term. A loose translation of the word is "summary," and it is just that—a summary of your qualifications, experience, and education that will benefit a prospective employer. You may have worked twenty years ago in a day care center, or you may direct your church choir, or you may have attended three colleges before you finally finished your degree, but is this information relevant to the position? If the answer is no, eliminate it. Employers who want more details will have you fill out an application, but the résumé itself should *not* include everything you've ever done.

Now it's time to turn to the nuts and bolts of the résumé by examining its various parts. You can refer to the two sample résumés at the end of the chapter to see how everything fits together.

Heading: At the top of the résumé place your name, address, zip code, and telephone number. If you have a work number that you're comfortable using, you can include that as well. You can center the heading, put it off to the left or the right, enlarge your name, or use lines or bullets. It should look professional, but that doesn't mean boring or predictable. Feel free to add a little flair. By the way—and this is very important—make sure you have an answering machine before you send out any résumés. If a prospective employer calls you and there's no one there, he or she will leave a message on the machine. If there's no machine, however, it's likely the caller will go on to the next name on the list and never call you back.

Objective (also called "Professional Objective" and "Career Objective"): This is where all that brainstorming in chapter 2 comes in handy. If you are able to narrow down a job objective, put one in; if you have a range of skills but don't want to limit yourself to one field, leave out the objective and summarize your qualifications under the profile (explained below). Keep the objective simple and direct and as specific as you can because it's the first thing anyone reads. For example, "Purchasing Manager" is good; "Purchasing Manager in a manufacturing environment" is better.

Profile (also called "Profile of Qualifications," "Summary," and "Highlights of Qualifications," among others): The profile is designed to summarize what you have to offer an employer. It's optional, but it's a good way to grab someone's attention and direct the focus of the résumé. This is also a good place to include your computer skills. The profile can be several bulleted points or a short paragraph, as illustrated below:

PROFILE **Management • Sales • Public Relations • Human Resources**

- Offer a broad spectrum of administrative experience in various organizational and business settings in the areas of management, labor relations, and program development.
- Proven ability to effectively sell ideas, concepts, and products. Developed and implemented a variety of successful marketing/sales and public relations activities.
- Background in the full supervision and development of large and diverse staffs.
- Familiar with a variety of computer software including WordPerfect 6.1, Lotus 1-2-3, dBase, and AmiPro.

Or:

PROFILE Widely experienced in vehicle maintenance, personnel supervision, and customer service accompanied by academic credentials in political science and intensive studies in engine power technology. Excellent investigative and problem-solving skills; good communication abilities in relating to people at all levels; effective in a high pressure, time sensitive environment. Computer literate.

Education: Name the schools you attended and any degrees you hold. Dates are optional, and if they go back too far, I recommend you not include them. If you have a bachelor's degree and an associate's degree, you should probably leave off the associate's degree unless it's in a field that is relevant to your objective and not covered under your bachelor's degree. Don't use the word *degree* on a résumé; instead, give your title ("Bachelor of Science in Accounting" not "Bachelor's Degree in Accounting").

If you don't have a degree, indicate any schooling or training you've completed. Information about your high school education is unnecessary if you have any college or additional training. Lead with your strengths; education comes first if it's especially significant, or if you're a new graduate. If you have more experience than schooling, lead with your experience. The exception is in medicine, law, and education, where it's common to lead with education. Some sample formats for education follow:

EDUCATION
Bachelor of Science in Accounting, 19–
BRADLEY UNIVERSITY—Peoria, IL

Or:

EDUCATION
All but one semester completed toward Bachelor of Science in Accounting
BRADLEY UNIVERSITY—Peoria, IL

Or:

EDUCATION
Studies in business and computer operations
ILLINOIS CENTRAL COLLEGE—East Peoria, IL

Or:

EDUCATION

Participated in numerous training programs including *Career Development for Managers, Data Communications, Disbursements & Procedures, Working in the Age of Diversity, Quality Service Every Time, Stress Management, Manager's Role as a Coach, In Search of Excellence,* and various computer seminars.

Experience (also called "Professional Experience" and "Employment History," to name a few): Give your title, the place of employment, the dates of employment, and a brief description of the work you've done for your current and previous positions. Remember to use action verbs and to write in the first person.

The problem with the experience section is that it can sound like a job description and easily become a tedious and boring read. To make it reflect more fully what *you* did in the position, rather than just provide a list of responsibilities, go back to your list of accomplishments (chapter 2) and incorporate them into your job description. Wherever you can, quantify with specific facts: Give the size of the facility you manage, the size of your inventory or budget, the percentage of sales increase, the number of clients you've generated for the company. Quantification lends credibility to the entire document. For example:

EXPERIENCE **Executive Director**   19– to Present
CBC LABOR COUNCIL—Bloomington, IL
Oversee full range of operations for the organization. Spearhead comprehensive marketing programs and multimedia advertising campaigns to promote positive labor-management relations. Draft grants, write press releases, and edit a biweekly newsletter. Organize conferences and sem-

inars, represent the organization to the public and the press, and develop public relations events. Hire, train, and supervise staff. Prepare and monitor annual budget.

Key Accomplishments:
- Provided leadership that resulted in CBC's recognition as a premier example of labor-management cooperation in the state by members of the governor's State Labor-Management Committee as well as various other labor-management councils.
- Increased membership and involvement of unions and contractor associations within the industry by 40 percent.
- Directed production of an economic development video and a school outreach video.
- Created comprehensive employee training manual.

Additional Heading: Other headings include "Honors and Awards," "Professional Associations," "Community Involvement," "Publications," "Certifications," and so on. In fact, the additional headings you can use are limited only by your imagination! Just make sure any information you include is relevant to the position for which you're applying, and keep it concise and to the point.

One of my favorite headings is "Endorsements" (also called "Sample Evaluation Comments"), which goes on the bottom of the résumé. If you have letters from supervisors, colleagues, or customers that are particularly glowing, you can quote excerpts from them on the résumé:

ENDORSEMENTS "Susan has stood in the direct firing line of adversarial forces and managed to mediate those divergent interests well." "One of her outstanding attributes is her ability to get jobs organized with a minimum of 'hassle.'" "A self-starter with initiative . . . intelligent and hard working." "Dealing with difficult people has become her specialty."

Personal: Leave off a "Personal" or "Interests" section with information about your family, age, weight, politics, religion, or hobbies. If you're looking for a position in outside sales, the fact that you play golf *might* be a plus. In most cases, however, putting personal information on a résumé is out of date and spells "dinosaur" to a hiring manager. Also, many employers prefer you not give them this information for fear of discrimination charges.

Tag Lines: You can round out your résumé at the bottom with the line "References Available on Request," although it's optional, and if lack of space gets to be a problem, you can do without it. Some other lines you might add are "Willing to Travel," "Willing to Relocate," "U.S. Citizen" (if there is any doubt), and "Portfolio Available on Request."

When you are finished, step back and look at your résumé. Look for a balanced, clear, and "reader friendly" document. Have someone you trust proofread it for you. I recommend you have it professionally printed using a laser or bubble jet printer, and that you use high quality paper. It need not be white; in fact, because white is so common, a little color and creativity may help your résumé stand out. There are hundreds of colors that are used for résumés including various shades of gray, sand, blue, and even mauve and salmon (although men or anyone in a conservative field should avoid even a hint of pink). Some newer résumé papers have creative borders and designs. Choose what you're comfortable with and what reflects who you are.

When sending a résumé in the mail, be sure it is accompanied by a cover letter (also called a "letter of introduction" or sometimes a "broadcast letter") that is typed and professional in both appearance and tone. If you drop off a résumé in person, a cover letter isn't mandatory (although it doesn't hurt to include it) because *you* are the cover. I recommend you use the heading that's on your résumé, and the same paper. This creates a "logo" of sorts that can be an effective marketing tool. Two sample cover letters are located at the end of the chapter.

A cover letter is usually broken down into three parts:

Introduction: If you've spoken to someone, or if you know the name of the person to whom you are sending the résumé, include the name along with the date. If you don't know a specific name, you can use a generic salutation such as "Ladies/Gentlemen" or "Allow me to introduce myself." (Avoid "Dear Sir" at all costs.) In the first paragraph, introduce yourself and indicate your interest in employment with the firm. Short and sweet, and pretty standard.

Body: This is the meat of your cover letter, and it's usually one or two paragraphs. Give a summary of your skills, and if you can target them to the company or the position, all the better. But please don't give a summary of your résumé. In a cover letter you have the opportunity to express yourself in a more personal manner than a résumé allows. You can emphasize your enthusiasm for computers, your willingness to learn, your interest in the company, or your philosophy of business or management or teaching. Don't wax on too much, however. The idea is to give the reader just enough information to pique his or her interest.

Conclusion: Again, the conclusion is pretty standard. Thank the reader for his or her time, *always* ask for an interview, and indicate that you will be following up at a later date if you do not receive a response.

Finally, always remember the cardinal rule of good writing is to keep it simple, direct, and concise. In what have been called the "63 words that could change the world," the late great William Strunk, professor of English at Cornell University, said it all:

> Vigorous writing is concise. A sentence should contain no unnecessary words, a paragraph no unnecessary sentences, for the same reason that a drawing should have no unnecessary lines and a machine no unnecessary parts. This requires not that the writer make all his sentences short, or that he avoid all detail and treat his subjects only in outline, but that every word *tell*.[3] (emphasis added)

Go back to this paragraph as you write your résumé and cover letter and ask yourself repeatedly: "What am I *telling* busy personnel directors who are eager to make a dent in a pile of résumés?" If the answer is nothing, or more than they care to know, or *less* than they need to know about how your abilities may benefit them, then edit your material accordingly until you get it right!

JOHN Q. PUBLIC
123 Forest Lane Indianapolis, IN 11111
Telephone (123) 456-7890

PROFILE

Offering a broad spectrum of experience in electronics, small machinery operations, sales, construction, customer relations, and staff supervision. History of progressing in responsibility and learning on the job, with little training necessary; excellent communication and problem-solving skills.

EXPERIENCE

Sales Manager   8/9- to Present
Building Materials Sales Representative   2/9- to 8/9-
SUPER HOME CENTER—Indianapolis, IN

As Sales Manager, supervise staff of eleven in the sales and installation of building materials. Coordinate crews for the installation of kitchens, bathrooms, electrical work, carpentry, and other projects. Interact extensively with customers, answering questions and resolving problems both over the phone and on site.

Began as Sales Representative: sold tools and home improvement products and gained extensive knowledge of lumber, tools, building, and hardware merchandise. Maintained inventory, set price controls, filled contractor orders, and arranged for pick up and delivery of merchandise.

Electronics Assembler/Tester   3/8- to 2/9-
SUMMER ELECTRONICS—Valparaiso, IN

Assembled electronic components for use in commercial and military aircraft. Followed blueprints in building cables from start to finish. Tested finished cables using both electronic voltage tests and computer checks, and reworked defective cables. Operated drill presses, braiding machinery, heat guns, soldering guns, and arber machines.

Sales Person/Installation/Warehouse Worker   6/8- to 1/8-
WATERBED WAREHOUSE—Indianapolis, IN

Began part-time while in the service; progressed to full-time. Performed a wide range of jobs including sales, customer service, warehousing, inventory management, and installation. Gained experience in the manufacturing and construction of waterbed products.

Aviation Ordinance Technician   10/8- to 11/8-
UNITED STATES NAVY—Omaha, NE

Performed aircraft and general shipyard maintenance and loaded and unloaded flight components in aircraft. Assistant welder and member of Flight Deck Fire Response Team.

EDUCATION

Advanced Electronics School
Aircraft Maintenance and Handling School
Fire Control School
UNITED STATES NAVY

– REFERENCES AVAILABLE ON REQUEST –

Shannon Smith

1234 W. Pine Avenue • Muncie, IN 44444 • (123) 555-7890

Objective   Elementary teacher for the hearing impaired

Summary
- Skilled in the use of a variety of effective teaching techniques including Cooperative Learning and Math Their Way.
- Able to adapt teaching styles to meet the needs of all students; employ constant, positive reinforcement to promote student success.
- Skilled in the use of *Kid Works 2* writing program and *Grandma & Me* interactive story. Also familiar with Microsoft Works word processing.

Education   **Bachelor of Science in Education**
Bachelor of Science in Special Education, Hearing Impaired
BALL STATE UNIVERSITY—Muncie, IN   5/9-

Certifications • State of Indiana Special Education/Hearing Impaired, K through 12
- State of Indiana Elementary Education, 1 through 6

Student Teaching   WASHINGTON ELEMENTARY—Farmington, IN   9/9- to 12/9-
Developed lessons and taught across the curriculum in a 3rd through 6th grade hearing impaired resource room. Implemented memory matching games for test reviews, original bulletin boards, and numerous creative learning activities. Also taught reading for advanced students in a 6th grade regular division classroom. Developed a number of learning activities around the novel *The Sign of the Beaver* including crossword puzzles for vocabulary, word searches, and journal writing.

SAUNDERS MIDDLE SCHOOL—Farmington, IN   8/9- to 10/9-
Taught 7th grade students in a hearing impaired, self-contained resource room. Worked with individual students, as well as with small groups.

Employment   **Private Tutor**   2/9- to Present
Teach two first graders twice a week.

Intramural Basketball Referee/Skills Instructor   1/9- to 4/9-
FARMINGTON COMMUNITY SCHOOLS—Farmington, IL

Swim Aide   6/9- to 7/9-
Clinic for Speech and Hearing Impaired Students
BALL STATE UNIVERSITY—Muncie, IN

Assistant Manager   4/9- to 7/9-
WRIGHT'S FAMILY ENTERTAINMENT—Farmington, IN

– References and Credentials Available on Request –

Steven L. Smith

XYZ Avenue
Peoria, IL 12345
Telephone: (321) 456-7890

July 22, 19–

Mr. John Jones
Human Resource Manager
Widget Manufacturing
Peoria, IL 12345

Dear Mr. Jones:

Thank you for speaking with me this afternoon regarding a welding and production position with your company. I am enclosing a copy of my résumé for your review and consideration.

My qualifications include extensive experience in welding, gas welding, machining, and brazing, as well as a strong background in repairing and maintaining all sorts of equipment. In addition to my skills, I learn fast, communicate well with co-workers, and enjoy taking on new challenges.

If you have an opening for a dependable, highly skilled employee who always tries to give 100 percent, I'd like to explore the possibility of employment with Widget Manufacturing.

I appreciate your time and interest in reviewing this material, and I look forward to speaking with you in the near future.

Sincerely,

Steven L. Smith

Steven L. Smith

Résumé enclosed

Sally J. Network

123 Ninth Street • Peoria, IL 12345 • (555) 456-7890

March 3, 19–

Allow me to introduce myself:

To express my interest in employment opportunities with your organization, I have enclosed a copy of my résumé. It will furnish you with specific information regarding my background.

As you will note, I offer eighteen years of progressive experience in sales and management, with a history of increasing market share and generating new business in each position I have held. I am a highly self-motivated individual with the ability to develop long-range sales strategies and effectively motivate both clients and personnel, and I have learned from experience that success lies in the extra effort. I am seeking a position in which my extensive background as a sales executive with a successful food broker will be of benefit, and I offer a commitment to the highest performance standards.

A résumé, of course, cannot take the place of a personal interview. Therefore, I would appreciate an appointment at your convenience to exchange additional information and discuss how my experience could be of value to your company.

Thank you for your time and professional courtesy in reviewing this material. I look forward to hearing from you.

Sincerely,

Sally J. Network

Sally J. Network

Résumé enclosed

4
The Search IS On

Generating Leads

First things first. Remembering that about 80 percent of all new jobs are not advertised, your initial priority is to generate a list of companies or organizations to approach for possible employment openings. Many people get to this point and flounder helplessly, but a focused and deliberate approach is likely to generate the success you're hoping to achieve.

I recommend you get a three-ring binder, prepare a page for each of the companies you contact, and keep the records in alphabetical order by company name. A card file is also a good way to do this, but if that's your choice, make sure you use large cards. The three by fives are likely to get too crowded.

You can start generating leads by simply calling the chamber of commerce for the city or cities where you're interested in working and asking to receive a list of major employers. Most chambers provide this service at no charge, or for a few dollars at most.

Next, pay a visit to your friendly reference librarian. Ask him or her for business books such as *Standard & Poor's Register of Corporations, Directors, and Executives*, or *The Job Hunter's Sourcebook: Where to Find Employment Leads and Other Job Search Resources*, or for specific job guides in your industry. A large library will also have telephone books from other cities. Plan to spend a day or more and bring your notebook with you. Write down not only names and addresses but relevant information about the various companies that interest you, including company history, structure, profits and losses, products, and specialties. Also note the names of division heads. Be sure to check out the information before you make any direct contacts as things can change by the time a book is published. A simple phone call to the company will allow you to verify details. When you begin to make contact, your knowledge of and interest in the company will help you stand out from the other candidates.

Don't limit yourself to large companies. Although the American dream is to work for the fortune 500s, it's a fact that the smaller and midsize companies are the ones that have experienced the most growth in recent years, while many larger companies have cut back.

In addition to library research, you'll want to develop leads through networking. This means contacting everyone you know who might know about a potential job . . . and everyone who might know of someone who might know about a potential job . . . You get the picture.

If you contact people by phone, write a short script ahead of time and practice it until it sounds natural. This may lack spontaneity, but believe me, the biggest complaint from those on the receiving end of this kind of call is that people tend to babble aimlessly. A busy employer does not want the task of helping you figure out what your skills are or what kind of job you're looking for, although he or she may be willing to assist you if you can provide the basic information. Here's where your list of skills and accomplishments will come in handy. You are sure to encounter the age-old statement "Tell me about yourself," and you will need to come up with an answer that's a little more concrete than "Well, I like people" or "I'm a hard worker," as valuable as those qualities are.

Keep your script short, pleasant, and concise. Tell the caller how you know him (if he isn't likely to recognize your name immediately), why you're calling, and what you have to offer. End the conversation by asking for something specific. For example:

Mr. Jones? This is Joan Johnson. I'm a friend of your daughter Sally, and I attend your church. In fact, my father sings with you in the choir. [Here he's likely to greet you and engage in some small talk. Be cordial but don't linger too long; his time is valuable, so progress steadily to the point.] I'm calling because I was recently laid off from Ace Plastics, and I'm looking for a job. I graduated from State University last year with a degree in public relations, and I worked as a marketing assistant at Ace for seven months. I have strong written and oral communication skills, and I'm familiar with a variety of word processing and graphics software. I'd be interested in a position in a similar field, or possibly an entry-level management opportunity. I was wondering, with your background in manufacturing, as well as your connection with area nonprofit organizations, if you could provide me with some contacts for possible job leads.

Don't be intimidated by this process; Mr. Jones is likely to be flattered that you called him. You may even consider ending the conversation by asking to meet with him to discuss his ideas about where you should proceed, in which case your last sentences may go like this:

> I was wondering if I could meet with you at your office, or perhaps somewhere for coffee. I promise I won't take up too much of your time, but with your background in manufacturing, as well as your contacts with area nonprofit organizations, I believe you'd be able to steer me in the direction of some valuable contacts and perhaps share some of your knowledge and experience that may be helpful to my job search.

You should remember one important rule of thumb, however: If you've asked for an informational meeting, *don't* use the time to ask for a job. That will only make you appear dishonest. If in the course of the conversation he mentions an opening with his company, you may say something like, "That sounds like a position that would interest me. Can you tell me how I might put in a formal application?" But if you've told him the meeting is for the purpose of getting leads and advice, don't take advantage of his generosity; stick to your agenda.

In addition to or instead of the phone calls, you may consider writing letters to people you know and including a self-addressed postcard for their reply. A sample letter appears on page 46.

Follow up on every lead, and don't forget to keep in touch with the people who have been kind enough to help you along the way. A thank-you note such as the one on page 47 is a thoughtful and professional courtesy that will go a long way in helping to build good will, and besides, it's a nice way of showing your appreciation. And it does not need to be typed; after all, it isn't a formal business letter, just a cordial thank-you.

Robert Johnson
123 Fourth Street • Anywhere, USA 12345 • (309) 555-1234

January 12, 19–

Jane Jones, Controller
Widget Manufacturing
567 Eighth Street
Somewhere, USA 23456

Dear Jane,

I haven't talked to you since you received your promotion, but I've heard that things have been going well for you and your family.

I'm writing to let you know that I was laid off due to recent cutbacks at Max Manufacturing. I have more than ten years of experience in operating and maintaining various types of equipment and machinery, and I also have a background in supervising and training workers.

I'd appreciate you sending me the names and addresses of two people whom I may contact for leads regarding machine operating or related supervisory positions in the manufacturing field. I know you're busy, so I've enclosed a self-addressed stamped postcard for your convenience.

Thanks for your help. I'll keep in touch and let you know how my job search is going.

Sincerely,

Bob Johnson
Bob Johnson

The classified section of your newspaper is one other source for employment information. By all means, if you see a job that interests you, send a résumé, give the employer a call, drop in, or all of the above. Ads are among the least effective means to finding a job, but that doesn't mean people are never successful when using them. Ads also serve as a good source for finding companies.

Let's say you'd love to work for Max Manufacturing, and one Sunday you spot an ad that says the company is seeking machine operators. But you're an administrative assistant, so you give a sigh and fold the paper and put it away—no openings for you there.

January 30, 19-

Dear Jane,

Just a note to thank you for the two leads you sent me. I've already spoken with Mr. Blount, and he has some openings coming up that look promising. I've written to Ms. McNamara and hope to hear from her soon.

I appreciate your help, and I'll let you know what happens.

Thanks again,
Bob

Wait a minute! If the company is hiring fifty machinists, perhaps there is some growth going on in that company. Add it to your list and note the advertisement that caught your eye. If a company is hiring at one level, there's a good chance it will be hiring at other levels as well.

Noticing trends in the classified section can also be helpful. What companies are hiring and what kinds of positions seem to be in the greatest demand? Ads can also tell you something about a company's history, always important to know when you land an interview. Does the ad say how long the company has been in business? Or perhaps something about its service or employee relations philosophy? Newspaper ads can give you all kinds of clues about the hidden job market, so check them faithfully.

Don't let the process of generating leads intimidate you. Many people will be glad to hear from you and will want to help. If they respond negatively, you haven't lost anything, and as long as you remain courteous, you have nothing to regret. Remember, the plan is to gain a broad base of contacts for possible employment. Continue to set goals for yourself, and continue plugging away.

5

"May I Have a Moment of Your Time?"

Telemarketing Your Way to Success

By now your three-ring binder is beginning to bulge with names of companies that may offer some possibilities. But following through on your leads involves a lot more effort on your part than sending your résumé. Your goal is to talk to as many hiring executives as possible, and the most effective tool you have in your job search repertoire is the telephone. In fact, it's been estimated that 70 percent of jobs are found through this kind of networking.

Your inclination may be to call personnel departments, but unless you're looking for a position in personnel, the people in that department do not have the power to hire you. More often than not, the personnel staff simply screens prospective hires for the company. There's also a pretty strong likelihood that if you call them and ask about any job openings, they will ask you to submit a résumé, which they can add to their burgeoning pile (sometimes known as "the black hole").

Copyright 1996 by Tom Cheney, reprinted with permission.

Personnel staff, secretaries, administrative assistants, receptionists, and switchboard operators often serve as gatekeepers: people who guard the people who have the power to hire you. Through your research, networking, and calling, hopefully you have learned the names of division heads or supervisors who will be doing the actual hiring. It will take some persistence, and you're guaranteed to run up against a few brick walls, but they're the ones you want to talk to. You should plan your calls early in the morning before the secretary gets in, later in the day after the secretary has left, or at lunchtime.

A word about secretaries: They are professionals who often have an extraordinary amount of influence. Get the name of each secretary you speak with if you can, and when you call back, address him or her by name. Be courteous and polite, but don't be too quick to say what you're calling about. If you say you're inquiring about possible employment openings, you may get rerouted back to the personnel department.

Give yourself a set number of phone calls to make each day; I recommend between ten and twenty. Make this a personal commitment, and if you're unemployed, think of it as your job. If you hold a position, this can be very difficult, but plan ahead, bring change, and call from a pay phone at lunchtime or during a break if you have to. The important thing is to set specific, achievable goals for yourself ("ten calls today") and to follow through with them. And don't let yourself fall into the trap of making the easy calls and ignoring the more difficult ones. You may enjoy calling old friends for the purpose of "networking" but dislike calling companies. Remember, it's important for you to do both.

To make the task of calling a little easier, prepare a short script. Include an introduction ("Ms. Roberts? My name is Sally Jenkins. I recently graduated from State University with a bachelor's degree in business administration"), a reason for the call ("I'm calling to inquire about possible employment openings with your company, either current or anticipated") and a short, polite question ("Do you have time to talk to me right now or would it be better for me to call you back later? What's the best time?"). And be ready to answer questions.

Your tone of voice should be confident, positive, friendly, and polite. Never, *never* issue demands, even indirectly ("I'm looking for a position where I'll be able to use more of my creative skills, but I won't do any weekend work and I must have at least a 10 percent increase over what I'm making now"). You'll have a chance to present and negotiate your concerns when you're a serious contender for a position, but if you start out with them, you won't get that far. Also, it's best not to leave messages on an answering machine. Your goal is to make direct contact, but you may be intercepted if your message gets there ahead of you.

Don't eat, chew gum, smoke, read, watch television, or, if you can help it, care for small children while you're making your calls, and tell your family that unless the house is on fire, you are not to be disturbed. If the idea of cold calling makes you nervous, it's a good idea to practice. Tape yourself engaging in a sample conversation, listen to how you sound, and enlist the advice of a friend. Remember to speak slowly and enunciate. Once you get started, it wouldn't be a bad idea to tape yourself during an actual phone conversation as well; then listen to yourself to make sure you sound natural and relaxed. The worst thing you can do when reading a script is to sound like you're reading a script! To avoid falling into the rut of sounding rehearsed, make regular, small changes in what you say.

If you're unsure of yourself, go over your script with an objective party. One prospective client called me recently to inquire about my services. He was looking for someone to type rather than write his résumé because, he told me, "I already done the résumé myself." If he talks like that on the phone to employers, he's likely to be making a lot of dead-end calls. A job seeker simply cannot afford grammatical gaffes, so if that's an area where you're weak, before you dial consult with someone whose judgment you trust.

Once you begin the phone work, you're sure to make a few mistakes. One client told me that for his first five or ten calls he was certain he sounded like he had mothballs in his mouth! Learn from your mistakes; do not let them discourage you.

You can move the conversation along and control its direction by asking questions about the company and possible openings. When doing this, try to avoid questions that can be answered with a simple yes or no because they're too easy to brush off. You may ask what kinds of openings are anticipated and when, or what steps you can take to improve your qualifications.

You will, of course, in spite of your best efforts and most flawless contacts, encounter rejection. But even then you may be able to generate some leads. Close the conversation by asking for the names of other division heads who may be hiring, or of people he or she knows in other companies who may be hiring. Don't prolong this; remember, employers are very busy and you don't want to overstay your welcome. Once you've been told no you may only get a chance to ask one question, so choose with care which one you want to ask. If the employer gives you any leads, ask if you can use his or her name, and make sure you follow up with a note of thanks. Then you can begin the process all over again by making another phone call that begins with: "Mr. Banks from ABC Widget Company [or from your marketing department] suggested that I call you . . ."

From my own experience, I have found that without exception my clients who are the most persistent and determined are the ones who are the most successful. This was confirmed by a human resource executive who was part of a human resource panel at a résumé writers' convention I attended.

The members of the panel represented several different industries and spoke on a variety of topics, including what they look for when they screen résumés, and tips on how to get through the maze of applicants. During an open discussion, one woman made a telling remark: "Please, *don't* tell your clients to send several résumés and call a lot of times. We just recently had an applicant who did that, and he was turned down by personnel at the same time another department hired him. It was so embarrassing."

You don't have to be a rocket scientist to understand what she was saying: Don't tell people to do this because it's an inconvenience to *us*. But in the same breath she admitted that it worked! And while I have all the respect in the world for human resource professionals, I do not work for them; I work for my clients. Therefore, I will continue to encourage job applicants to be persistent and indefatigable.

A final warning: Prepare yourself for rejection. You may receive a negative response as much as 90 percent of the time! Remember to keep telling yourself that for every no you hear you are just that much closer to the right yes. The nature of this work is enough to discourage anyone, and this is a real catch-22 because if you get discouraged, you are not likely to be successful. So set your goals, understand that rejection isn't personal, learn from your mistakes, and resolve to keep plugging away.

6

Whatsoever Things Are Good

Keeping Your Eye on the Prize

We'd like you to come in for an interview tomorrow at 3 o'clock," said the efficient voice on the other end of the phone. I was not given any options. She said it was for an office job, and I was looking for a management-level position, but I was unemployed and feeling slightly desperate. I told her I'd be there.

When I arrived, the receptionist coldly gave me a form to fill out, and I found my way to a dusty seat in the lobby, which was undergoing extensive renovation. In a short while a man came out to speak with me. He didn't introduce himself; he didn't sit down; he didn't invite me into his office; he didn't shake my hand; and he didn't look me in the eye. We remained in the lobby, filled with construction workers, hammering, and general chaos, during the course of the interview.

"Your résumé doesn't show that you have any book-keeping experience," he said tersely. It sounded like more of an accusation than an inquiry. Of course I don't have any bookkeeping experience, I thought. I'm an

English major; I hate numbers. I can't even balance a checkbook!

"I have office and computer experience," I told him, "and I have good communication skills, but I've never done any bookkeeping." I was using my most polite tone of voice. I had come a long way for this interview, and I really needed a job.

He began firing off bookkeeping questions, none of which I could answer, and I felt like an idiot. He was annoyed because I was clearly a waste of his time. It apparently did not occur to him that someone in the company, with my résumé in hand, had called *me* in for this interview under the pretext that the job was something other than what it was, and that *my* valuable time was being wasted as well.

I alternated between crying and yelling all the way home. I had worked so hard to earn this shiny new degree, which at this point didn't seem to be worth the paper it was printed on. I was too old; I was too inexperienced; my degree was in the wrong field; I was overqualified; I was underqualified. I felt like a long-distance runner who had come up against the proverbial "wall" and would never get past it. My self-esteem, sense of security, and general energy and enthusiasm were seriously eroding.

Sound familiar? It seems as if everyone who's been job hunting in the past decade has had a similar experience, accompanied by feelings of humiliation, self-doubt, and discouragement, and has felt like giving up. These feelings are only intensified if you're also unemployed, or if you've recently been let go from a position.

As the rejection letters come in, some of them polite and encouraging ("Your qualifications are impressive but . . .") and some of them curt and to the point ("Your qualifications do not match our needs . . ."), the feelings of discouragement mount. Don't take it personally, all the books say, but that can be mighty difficult after a while. The frustration can undo even the most well-planned job search if you let it.

There are a lot of standard remedies for making it over the wall, and they run the gamut from exercise to meditating to saying positive things to yourself. Yes, there are authors and career counselors who advise job seekers to talk to themselves. "I am a valuable person." "I have many talents." "I am loved and important to a number of people." "I am bright and competent and an employer is going to be lucky to get me."

While it's certainly important to maintain your self-esteem, I'm inclined to believe that the artificially manufactured variety is likely to fall short of the mark. The Bible has a much better way.

Paul finished his upbeat letter to the church at Philippi with some good and timely advice. "Whatever is true, whatever is noble, whatever is right, whatever is pure, whatever is lovely, whatever is admirable—if anything is excellent or praiseworthy—think about such things. . . . And the God of peace will be with you" (Phil. 4:8–9).

If you are between jobs, it's likely you have some extra time on your hands, even if you're launching an aggressive job search campaign. That time can be a blessing or a curse. If you use it to catch up on soap operas and lost sleep, you're likely to slide quickly into a pit of depression and discouragement.

Or perhaps you're overworked at the job you have and you can barely find time to make a few calls and send out a résumé or two in any given week. What time you do invest seems to be getting you nowhere, and you're wondering if you'll ever get off the merry-go-round.

The demands for your attention may be very compelling and the blows to your ego may seem overwhelming, but whatever your situation, the Word of God beckons you to step back and see the big picture. Do not become bogged down in bitterness and recriminations, however tempting they may be, or in guilt and self-doubt, or in reliving the past or worrying about the future. Doing so will only sabotage your job search, hurt your family, and most important, run a wedge between you and the Lord when you should be drawing nearer to him.

It is a great irony that Paul wrote his letter to the church at Philippi from a prison cell while he was awaiting death. One might expect the tone to be sad and somber, but that was far from the case. Philippians has been called "the joy book," and it is filled with a spirit of determination and even delight in the face of great personal adversity.

Paul says, "Rejoice in the Lord always. I will say it again: Rejoice!" (Phil. 4:4). And then he tells us how: "Do not be anxious about anything, but in everything, by prayer and petition, with thanksgiving, present your requests to God. And the peace of God, which transcends all understanding, will guard your hearts and your minds in Christ Jesus" (Phil. 4:6–7).

So take a long walk and breathe in deeply, and thank God for the beauty of his creation. Get up an hour early and spend extra time in prayer and Bible study. By all means bring your concerns and petitions to God, but don't forget to praise and thank him as well. Count your blessings. Thank him for your family, your friends, your home, your church, not to mention his Word and his love for you. Thank him in advance for providing and getting you through this time in your life, because he will, whether you happen to believe it at the moment or not. Ask him to fill you with his peace and to enable you to trust him for each day.

Many people have told me that to their amazement a time of unemployment and career transition turned out to be a time of tremendous spiritual growth and renewal. I know that was the case in my life. After I cried and lamented my personal fate, I went running like a little child into the arms of the Father. During that period in my life, I learned to depend on God in ways that all my experience in more than twenty years as a Christian had not taught me. I spent more time in prayer and I savored the Word in new ways. In fact, I underlined and dated passages in the Bible, and to this day I go back to them and marvel at how God has kept his promises.

I recommend that you make an extra effort during this time of transition to draw closer to the One who created you for himself. After all, growing in Christ is the primary purpose we were put on this planet. You may suffer indignities, frustrations, disappointments, and uncertainties as you maneuver the road before you, but they will pass. Remember that your value does not lie in your position or your paycheck, and that your safety and security come ultimately and only from God. You are not your job title, your business, or your field of study. You are a beloved child of the Father. Keep your eyes fixed on those things that are true and noble and lovely, and the God of all peace will guard your heart and mind in Christ Jesus.

He really will.

7

Employment Agencies and Headhunters

Finding Your Way through the Jungle

There's a saying in the employment industry: Agencies and recruiters do not find jobs for people, they find people for jobs. In other words, with very few exceptions, they don't work for you, they work for the employer. Since people in this business are normally paid on a commission basis, it is a volume industry that usually has a rapid turnover of clients.

Among employment agencies, there are those for both permanent and temporary employees. In the past, temporary agencies placed primarily clerical and blue-collar workers, but that's no longer the case. Companies have become increasingly cost conscious in recent years and more reticent about taking on full-time workers who are unproven. Consequently, the temporary worker has become the norm in many organizations, from entry-level clerical jobs to management positions, and everything in between. Many agencies even offer benefits to their temporary workers.

The problem with a temporary agency is obvious, however: a lack of job security. Nevertheless, if you've been looking for a while with no success, you may want to consider this option. Temporary assignments allow you to fill in gaps in your résumé, provide you with valuable experience, and enable you to make new contacts. It's even possible that a temporary job will lead to something permanent.

Private agencies that place people for permanent positions charge a fee, often a percentage of the first year's salary. Sometimes the fee is paid by the employer, sometimes by the employee, and sometimes it's divided between the two.

People looking for jobs normally contact these agencies in response to a newspaper ad, and some companies regularly use certain agencies. The agencies screen prospective employees, perform reference checks, and generally save companies a great deal of time and money, while only about 5 percent or less of the people who walk into employment agencies hoping to find a job ever do. Clearly this is a service of significant benefit to the *employer*, even though you may be the one who foots the bill. So before you go for an interview, understand the fee arrangement. If the fee is not paid by the employer, make sure you're willing and able to pay it in full if you accept an offer. It could be hundreds if not thousands of dollars.

To help you determine if you are working with a stable and reputable employment agency, ask how long it has been in business, not just as a nationwide chain, which some are, but how long it has been in your area. Franchise offices may be of particular benefit if you're looking to relocate. Ask your employment counselor how long he or she has been with the company and how long he or she has been an employment counselor. Since these are commission jobs, there can be a great deal of turnover.

One of my clients had an experience in which he went to an agency, filled out the forms, took the tests, submitted to a screening interview, and called back a week later only to find out the counselor who had interviewed him had left, and no one there could find the client's records.

Of course, there are a number of highly reputable agencies, as well as competent and caring professionals in the field. Indications of stability include the CPC designation (Certified Personnel Consultant), and membership in the National Association of Personnel Consultants or the National Association of Temporary Services, professional organizations for the industry.

In addition to employment agencies, there are thousands of recruiters nationwide, also known as executive search firms and "headhunters." Many of them specialize in placing professionals in mid- to upper-level positions, which means that blue-collar and clerical workers, as well as new grads, are likely to be wasting their time when approaching these firms. In addition, if you're changing careers (say you've been a retail manager for fifteen years and you'd like to get into public relations), you would not be a good candidate for this kind of service because recruiters are looking for people who are accomplished in a specific field. Remember, the emphasis is on volume, so for the most part they're looking for applicants they can place quickly and with relative ease.

Executive search firms are paid by the employer and fall under two categories. About 20 percent are "retained" firms, which conduct personnel searches for companies and are paid whether they place a candidate with the employer or not. The rest are "contingency" firms, and they're paid only when they forward a client to an employer who is then hired.

Executive search firms often get hundreds of résumés every week that they cannot use. If you approach them, do so as you would a prospective employer. Make sure your résumé and cover letter are polished and professional, and if you get an interview, dress the part and be prepared. If you're interested in this type of service, you can purchase the *Directory of Executive Recruiters* by writing Consultant News, Templeton Road, Fitzwilliam, New Hampshire 03447, or by calling 1-800-531-0007.

To round things out, about two thousand local state employment offices, sometimes called "Job Service," exist throughout the country. These offices are part of a nationwide federal network called The United States Employment Service (USES). Most of them provide assistance to workers at a variety of levels—blue-collar, clerical, management—and they have access to job listings. Some people have found these services to be of help. They're worth checking out, though their success rate has been estimated at only about 10 to 15 percent at the most.

Since your chances of finding a job through an agency or a headhunter are remote (you are likely to have better odds with the want ads), don't invest a disproportionate amount of your time and resources in this area. If you learn of a job that interests you through an agency, or if you learn of a recruiter who may have some good leads, by all means look into it, but keep the main focus of your job search on networking, calling, and following up. These techniques are far more likely to prove successful.

8

Don't Get Caught without Backup

Supplying References

Sam was clean and polished, and he made sure he arrived at the interview on time—not too early, certainly not late. He had practiced his answers to a hundred questions, and he was sure he was ready for anything. Things began swimmingly. He was charming and polite, and he had researched the job and the company enough to know what the prospective employer was looking for in an employee. He was just beginning to think the job was in the bag when the interviewer asked to see his references.

"References? Uh, well, uh . . . Can I send them to you?"

This is a scenario you want to avoid. People make a number of mistakes with regard to their references. They may send them too early or, like our friend Sam, be unprepared when asked to supply them. Other common mistakes include using too many references, or too few, or the wrong references, or giving too little information about them, or too much.

You may be inclined to use a next-door neighbor, or a family friend, or even your minister, but these are personal references, and they don't carry as much weight as professional references. Employers do not want to hear what a nice person you are. They want to hear that you are competent and hardworking and have the skills to do the job. And, of course, this is most likely to come from someone you've worked with in the past. This may be your minister if you've held some leadership roles in your church, or someone from an organization in which you've been involved.

You will need at least three references and no more than five or six. Supervisors and managers are the best people to list as references, or teachers, if you've recently completed school. It's also acceptable to use people with whom you've done business: a banker, a customer, or a colleague. You may even use people you've supervised, although it would be best to at least lead with someone who supervised you.

Choose people who are likely to say great things about you and who can convey those things over the phone or in a letter. If your last manager thinks you can leap tall buildings with a single bound but he speaks in a monotone and tends to be inarticulate, he may not be the best person for people to contact.

Of course, you will need to contact in advance the people you have chosen to ask if you may use them as references, and don't be afraid to remind them of your accomplishments and to suggest things you'd like them to highlight if they get a call. Also, it's not a bad idea to ask an employer when you leave a job if you may have a letter of recommendation. Even if your leaving was awkward or unpleasant, if there's someone in the company with whom you've remained on positive terms, ask that person for a letter. This will give you something constructive to show a future employer if there are any questions about why you left. Hold on to these letters and be prepared to give copies to an interviewer if the subject comes up. If the letters are particularly glowing, you may want to incorporate brief quotes from them into your résumé, either under a separate heading called "Endorsements" or under your work experience. It's normally preferable to leave your references off your résumé. You are likely to be sending your résumé to a number of people, and it's not a good idea to invite someone to contact your references until you've established a mutual interest with an employer, usually during an interview. There are exceptions, of course. The traditional curriculum vitae, normally used by people in higher education and the medical field, does include references at the end, but even the CV has gone through an evolution of sorts. These days it's not uncommon for a curriculum vitae to resemble a standard résumé.

Once you have a list of references, you need to organize them and present them in a professional manner. They should be listed on a separate sheet of paper with your name and address at the top, the title REFERENCES or PROFESSIONAL REFERENCES under that, followed by the references themselves. Lead with the most positive and impressive. People often call one or two references and leave it at that, so you want them calling your best first.

When listing a reference, include the name, making sure it is spelled correctly, the title, the place where he or she works, an address (either business or home), and his or her business phone, home phone, or both. It's very important that you give some indication as to how you know each reference. For example, if your number one reference, Linda Smith, was your supervisor when you worked at Class Video but she's now moved to Action Pharmaceuticals, you can indicate this in the following way:

Linda Smith
Administrative Assistant, Action Pharmaceuticals
Former Supervisor, Class Video
Street Address
City, State, Zip
Phone with area code

Always bring your references with you to an interview, either in a file folder or a briefcase. (Briefcases are a nice touch for office and professional jobs but a bit much if you're applying for a blue-collar position.) If the interviewer asks for your references, you'll be prepared. If he or she does not, I recommend you end the interview by offering them. You may say, "Thank you for your time. Before I leave, I'd like to give you a list of my references. If you have any questions, I hope you'll feel free to contact them."

If other candidates are interviewing for the same position, you're the one who left something, and you're the one who invited the employer to check up on you. This is a very confident, professional gesture, and it will make you stand out from the other job seekers.

9

Are You Worth Your Weight in Gold?

Responding to Salary Questions

You're lounging around your living room on a Sunday afternoon scanning the want ads when you see an advertisement for a position that is perfect for you. With nothing to lose, you decide to send a résumé the following morning. But there's a problem: They ask you to send a salary history as well. And you wonder, What in the world is a salary history, and why do they want to see one?

A salary history is just what the title implies. It's a history of your salary progression, usually going back about five years. Potential employers ask to see your salary history because they're looking for two things: They want to see if there's been progression (presumably if you began at $18,000 four years ago and you're now making $30,000, you've done well), and they want to see what you're making at the present time.

If you decide to send a salary history, there are several ways you can do it. You can send it on a separate sheet, something like your reference list, or you can incorporate it into your cover letter. If you list your salary history on a separate page, you can give a year-by-year account of your history beginning with the current year and working backward. For example:

SALARY HISTORY

19–: $32,000

19–: $30,000

19–: $26,500

19–: $22,000

19–: $20,500

Or you can list the most recent companies where you've worked and give your beginning and ending salary with each one, like this:

SALARY HISTORY

Widget Manufacturing, 19– to Present
$22,000 to $29,000

Ace Production Company, 19– to 19–
$16,750 to $23,000

You can also add at the bottom of the page "Salary is negotiable" and/or "Salary includes bonuses" if you like. Or, to make things much easier, you can add a note to your cover letter that answers salary questions: "With regard to your request for a salary history, I have been working for Ace Equipment Company for six years, where I have progressed from $18,000 to my current salary of $26,000."

I used to prepare salary histories for people all the time, but I rarely do them anymore because I believe they're likely to do more harm than good. The only reason people ask to see your salary history is because they're looking for an excuse to screen you out. Remember that it's not uncommon for employers to get hundreds of responses to one ad, so they are looking for anything that will make their job easier in narrowing down the number of candidates to consider.

Let's say you're making $35,000 a year and the job for which you're applying pays $25,000. You *may* be willing to come down somewhat in salary, and if they meet you,

$25,000--
AS IS.

By permission of H. L. Schwadron.

they *may* like you enough to negotiate a little bit. But you'll never get that chance if they see your current salary. "Too expensive for us," they'll say, and if you're lucky, you'll get a polite letter about being "overqualified."

Or you may be making $25,000 a year while they're offering $35,000. If you tell them what you make, they're likely to decide you're making too little and they don't want to give you that much of a raise. Either they'll lower the salary to fit you (something you would prefer to avoid), or they'll give your résumé the heave-ho and move on to "more qualified" candidates. Either way, you have a strike against you before you begin.

You may also run into a problem if your salary history shows some dips. For example, perhaps you made $30,000 five years ago and now you're making $18,000. You may have a very good reason for this. Perhaps you changed careers and willingly took a cut in pay to get into another field, or you lost a job through no fault of your own and were forced to take a cut, or you may have left a high stress job for a less demanding position because of family responsibilities. But if they see the drop in salary, it will be a red flag: "What is wrong with this person?" You're better off not revealing that information until you have had the chance to speak to them in person. Then if you're asked, keep your explanation as brief and to the point as you can, and whatever you do, *don't* get into a long story about your previous jobs, much less your personal life.

For example, you can say, "At that time I had some pressing family responsibilities that demanded my attention. Since then things have straightened out and I'm ready to get back to something more challenging." Or, "You may have heard of the cutbacks at Widget Manufacturing two years back. My position was one that was eliminated, so I took my most recent job to tide me over, but I'm ready to get back to something more challenging." Or, "I did very well in retail, but I was interested in getting into graphic design. I decided to make a change so I could gain some broader experience." You get the picture.

Salary questions present another problem: It's quite presumptuous for a total stranger to ask you to hand over a salary history, and many people are uncomfortable divulging something so personal. This is particularly difficult when responding to a blind ad because you have no idea who will be seeing it. Presumably the recipients will be discreet, but you have no guarantee.

I recommend you respond to such queries in the cover letter. You don't want to ignore the request for a salary history, but you don't want to give it to them either, at least not at this point. You may say something like: "With regard to your request for a salary history, I would be happy to provide one once we have established a mutual interest." Then bring it with you to an interview, but don't offer it unless you're asked. That way you don't limit your options before you get in the door.

Of course, some employers are very stubborn on this point. I've had a few managers tell me they won't even consider a candidate without a salary history, so it *may* cause more harm to exclude it. To make your own judgment, you will need to weigh the information you have about the company, your knowledge of salary expectations in your field, and how your history will fit into the overall picture. If you're unsure, leave it out.

There's another salary question that comes up, sometimes in an ad, sometimes over the phone, and sometimes during an interview: What salary are you looking for?

Red light! The same rule applies here. If your figure is too low or too high, you may limit your opportunities or put yourself out of the running. Remember, questions about salary are almost always asked to screen you out.

If you're speaking to someone, you can ask the salary range for the position. But I would caution that if you ask this question, you may get into a cat and mouse game where the person throws it back on you: "First I want to know what your expectations are." Then you're stuck, and unless you're very clever, you'll have to give an answer. If he or she does quote a figure, you can simply respond that the figure is in your ballpark, or that it's within a negotiable range.

When responding to this question in a letter, you can say you're open to negotiation with regard to salary, and that your primary concern at this point is the challenge and opportunity the job offers. It's a nice way of changing the subject while demonstrating your interest in the position and the company. It also prevents you from shooting yourself in the foot by quoting a figure that will limit your chances—or take you out of the running altogether.

Think through the salary question before it's asked, and remember when you encounter any inquiries about salary to proceed with caution.

10

You're On!

Succeeding at the Interview

You've completed your personal inventory, you've prepared your résumé, you've done the research, you've developed leads, you've gotten your references together, and you've called and dropped in on more people than you can count. Finally it happens: The phone rings and you're asked if you can come in for an interview. Now you can understand what a Hollywood hopeful feels like when contacted about that all-important audition! In fact, an interview is an audition of sorts, offering you a chance to try out for what may be the part you've been waiting for.

Books and articles on various interviewing techniques abound. As with anything else, some of them are helpful and some of them are not. There are two recurring mistakes. First, some authors encourage job seekers to memorize canned answers in response to every conceivable interview question. Interviewers are not stupid, and unless you're very good at sounding natural and spontaneous when you're not being natural and spontaneous, this may very well blow up in your face. Second, a number of interview books encourage job seekers to say whatever is necessary to secure an offer. Once you've been offered the job you have the option to say no, but until then the strategy is to say whatever the interviewer wants to hear.

For example: "Are you willing to work weekends?"

"Absolutely," you are to say with boundless energy and sincerity. "My dedication to the job is so great that my family, my friends, and everything I believe in take a back seat. I'll work a hundred hours every week if it's necessary. I'll travel, I'll relocate, I'll sell my mother. Anything you want, I'll do it."

That may be a slight exaggeration, but only slight. Some books and interview coaches encourage job seekers to go well beyond the normal flexibility expected of a serious candidate and to promise just about anything. Inherent in this is the assumption that the interview is a one-way street in which you alone, the job candidate, must prove yourself worthy of a given job. On the contrary! The interview is a two-way street, and it gives you an opportunity to determine whether you want to work for this employer and this company. Remember that. Just as you are wondering whether you will get the all-important offer, the interviewer may be wondering what it will take to get you to say yes. Just as you hope to sell yourself to the company, the company must also sell itself to you.

This isn't to say that you shouldn't prepare for an interview. There are many details you will need to think about, from the minute the phone rings, and even before.

Clothes don't "make the man," regardless of what the cliché says, but what you wear to an interview will influence how you are perceived. It's a good idea to dress a notch above what you'd normally wear on the job. For office and professional positions, both men and women should wear a suit, preferably dark in color and somewhat conservative, no ostentatious jewelry, and no cologne or perfume. If you're applying for a blue-collar or fast-food position, you can dress down a bit, but leave the jeans with the holes in them at home.

Do as much research on the company as you can before the interview. Stop by the library and look for related articles in newspapers or magazines, call the chamber of commerce, and talk to anyone and everyone you may know who works there. Learn about what they do, the company's history, the corporate structure, and their way of doing business. During the interview, you will be able to ask intelligent questions, and as the conversation progresses, it will demonstrate your interest in the company, something employers like to see. And bring several copies of your résumé with you to the interview, along with your references, of course. You never know when you might have more than one interviewer, or an interview panel. It's a professional gesture on your part to be able to offer copies of your résumé to each of your interviewers in case they don't have them.

While canned answers are out, you would do well to go over a list of possible interview questions and think about how you may answer them. The traditional interview includes general subjective questions: Tell me about yourself, what are your greatest strengths, what are your greatest weaknesses, and so on. It's easy to begin rambling when answering questions of this nature. Make sure you keep your answers reasonably short, and relate them to business. If you're applying for a job as an accountant, and you say that your greatest strength is your parenting skill—as important as that is—you are not likely to score any points.

Succeeding at the Interview

Regarding the "greatest weaknesses" question, the traditional (and *very* canned) response is to take a strength and disguise it as a weakness. For example, you may say, "I'm a perfectionist" or "I'm a workaholic" or "I'm always early and most days I start work an hour ahead of time." These answers are from the-interviewer-is-an-idiot school of thought, and they aren't likely to fool anyone. You'd be better off mentioning a genuine weakness that you've recognized and made progress in overcoming. For example, "I've had trouble delegating work, but with recent cutbacks we've all been overloaded. So I implemented team meetings and cross training, and I've had to learn to trust the people under me. To my surprise, production has gone up and morale is improved. It can be a blow to the ego to discover that you're not the only competent person in the office, but it was something I needed to learn. I think it's made me a better manager."

This tells an interviewer three things: You're not perfect (actually, he or she already knew that), you're honest, and you're able to acknowledge your weaknesses and learn from them.

Alas, most interviewers are managers who have little or no interviewing training and even less interviewing proficiency. But there are some interviewing techniques that are intense and effective and for which you would do well to be prepared, just in case you do meet up with a skilled interviewer.

Rather than ask subjective questions, some interviewers probe for an objective understanding of what you've accomplished and what your capabilities are. They aren't looking for general answers—"I'm good with people," "I pick up computer software easily," "I'm an open supervisor." They are looking for specific examples of your performance relating to the job. *How* are you good with people? *What* computer software do you know? *Give an illustration* of how you are an open supervisor. You will be asked to provide specific examples to back up what you say.

For example, if the job requires problem-solving skills, you will be asked to give an illustration of when and how you solved a problem. Without lingering over extraneous details, you need to be as concrete as possible. Describe the problem and talk about how you approached it, how you resolved it, and what the repercussions were. You may also be asked to describe a mistake you made. Again, go through the process (don't try to say you never made a mistake) and indicate how you handled it and what it taught you. If the interviewer presses for more and more mistakes or weaknesses, however, respond by saying you can't think of any more. This is a ploy used by some interviewers designed to uncover weak areas, so don't talk yourself into a corner.

It's not enough to have a general idea of what your skills are; you must be able to give examples of how you *used* those skills. During the stress of an interview, you may find yourself unable to think of what you want to say. Plan ahead! Write down your answers to the following questions, and remember to be specific.

1. When and how did you solve a problem relating to your job? What were the results?
2. Give an example of a project or idea that you had to convince someone else to support. How did you do it? Detail your strategy. What were the results?
3. Tell of a time you had to deal with an angry customer. How did you respond?
4. Were you ever in a situation at work where you experienced a conflict with another worker? What caused it and how did you deal with it?

5. Were you ever in a situation at work where you experienced a conflict with your boss? What caused it and how did you deal with it?
6. Tell me about a time when you saw what needed to be done and did it without having to be told.
7. Give an example of a mistake you made on the job. How did you handle it? What did you learn?
8. Give an example of a time when you had to make a decision between two equally good (or equally bad) choices. How did you make your decision?
9. Tell me something that you've done at work in the past year or two that you're really proud of.
10. Tell me something that you've done at work in the past year or two that you wish you'd done differently.

Some additional questions may be: Did you ever have to fire anyone? Give an example of when you've been a part of a team. Tell me about a project you managed. Questions for managers may include: What is your supervisory style? Give an example of how you handled a conflict and delegated responsibility. Or you may be asked specific questions relating to the position for which you're applying regarding technical skills or job knowledge. Write down five more questions you think you may be asked, and then write your answers.

This exercise is important whether your interviewer is vague or specific, subjective or objective, skilled or unskilled. The more specific and concrete you can be in answering any questions, and the more you can relate your answers to your performance on the job, the better. A word of caution: Never, never tell a lie, no matter what. Lies will come back to haunt you, guaranteed.

It's also a good idea to go through a mock interview with a friend ahead of time and videotape the process. You may notice something in your presentation that needs improvement, so give it a try. You want to demonstrate poise, eye contact, confidence, and good posture. Some qualities that personnel managers have told me turn them off in an interview include fawning, groveling, arguing, being condescending, getting defensive, making demands, or becoming too chummy or familiar. Watch carefully to see that you accentuate the positive and eliminate the negative.

And speaking of downplaying the negative, don't speak disparagingly about a former employer. When pressed as to why you left a position, you may mention a difference in philosophy, or possibly a "personality conflict," but couch all negative comments in positive remarks: "I learned a lot from that company, and during my four years there I developed some valuable skills. I'm grateful for the opportunity, and if you'd like, I can give you the names of some people to contact there for references. However, in the last year there were some management changes and a new boss. He and I had some different ideas about how to relate to customers. I'm just more hands-on, and I believe in trying to resolve problems before they begin. He didn't want me to spend so much time in customer support. After giving it some serious consideration, I felt it was time to leave."

If you're in a technical or creative field, using a portfolio is one way to help control the focus of the interview and gear it toward your abilities. This may include pictures of products you helped design, samples of artwork you've prepared, or flyers you've created, as well as accompanying awards. Put everything together in a notebook, note on your résumé that you have a portfolio available, and bring it with you to an interview. After the introductions, mention that you have a portfolio with samples of your work if the interviewer is interested. Usually during the course of an interview you'll get a chance to make a presentation. I've heard of teachers, graphic artists, and even sales representatives using portfolios successfully in interviews. I had one hiring manager tell me that his most memorable interview was with an engineer who stood out from the others with an impressive portfolio. It worked—he got the job.

Toward the close of the interview you will probably be asked if you have any questions. You may be tempted to ask about benefits and overtime, but you're likely to make more of a hit if you express an interest in the company and the position. Thoughtful questions focus on who you would be working for, the company's organization chart, the company history, how many candidates are being considered for the position, what qualifications they're looking for, whether this is a new position, and if it's not, why the previous person left. It's also acceptable to ask how long an interviewer has been with the company, as well as what he or she likes about working there or *doesn't* like about the company. You may also ask to speak with other people in the department with whom you would be working, particularly if this is your second or third interview with the same company.

As the interview comes to a close, don't hesitate to say that you're very interested in the position if, in fact, you are. Then be sure to ask the final two-part question: "When do you expect to make a decision?" and "When can I expect to hear from you?" If the interviewer says "within the next ten days" and you haven't heard anything in two weeks, you are perfectly justified in calling, and I strongly recommend that you do. This indicates your continuing interest and keeps your name on the front burner in case for some reason they're dragging their feet on the decision. Finally, before you leave, get the name (correctly spelled) and title of everyone who interviewed you. They should all receive a thank-you note from you within a few days.

You remember thank-you notes. Every Christmas your mother hounded you until you got them all written, and if you didn't get them done, they hung over your head like the sword of Damocles. Thank-you notes are a simple courtesy, one that, like so many others, has fallen by the wayside in recent years. It's time to dust them off and give them a new life.

Thank-you notes are recommended by books and career counselors both far and wide, but the fact of the matter is very few people write them. I had a principal tell me that in fifteen years of interviewing teachers he had never received a thank-you note. If teachers don't write them, nobody does. Except for new grads, that is. I'm finding that many college graduates have been indoctrinated by their schools to write thank-you letters. Universities are working harder than ever to give their graduates a competitive edge, and one way to do that is with the thank-you note. If you're in sales or a professional field, it may be expected of you. If you're a blue-collar worker, it's still a nice touch and is guaranteed to make you stand out from the pack. Writing a thank-you note after an interview demonstrates initiative, follow-through, and professionalism. You simply cannot afford not to.

Your note can be typed or handwritten. After all, it's a thank-you note, not a formal business letter, although if you write it out by hand, make sure it's neat and use black ink. You may want to write it on stationery designed to match your résumé. It should begin, of course, by thanking the interviewer for his or her time and for the information you gained about the company and the job during the interview. Follow that by referring to something that was mentioned in the interview, something about the company or the position that sounded particularly positive. It may be the teamwork in the shop, the fact that the company is growing, the commitment to customer support, or the challenge of the position.

This gives you a perfect lead to tell the interviewer one more time how wonderful you are! Make sure to point out how your qualifications fit with the position at hand. You may also want to address a weakness that came up in the interview. For example, you could say, "I realize I do not have any actual experience in your particular windows program, but I've used WordPerfect for windows for two years, and I've taught myself several other systems as well, including Lotus, AmiPro, and Harvard Graphics. I have no doubt I could be up to speed on your system within a very short time."

Thank-you notes have the highest impact the sooner they are received, so make sure you get your letter in the mail the day of the interview or the following day, no later. You want the note to get to the employer while the momentum is on your side. If he or she hears from you within a day or two, you may still be in his or her thoughts. If you don't send the letter for a week, the interviewer may no longer even remember who you are.

Refer to the sample thank-you note on page 82, but don't copy it word for word. See to it that your letter speaks to the interview, the company, and the job, and is as individualized as possible.

If you get turned down for a position, you may want to contact the person with whom you spoke and, in as cordial and nonthreatening a tone as possible, ask if he or she may be able to make some suggestions as to how you can improve your candidacy, or even your interviewing skills. There may be some mistakes you're making in interviews that you aren't even aware of. Sometimes an interviewer will be willing to give some advice, and it's worth asking. This also indicates your interest in self-improvement, and who knows, they may think

Shawn Donaldson
89 Tenth Street
Anytown, USA 34567
(123) 456-7890

July 1, 19–

Emily Frederickson, Service Manager
XYZ Service Corporation
55 Service Boulevard
Sometown, USA 45678

Dear Emily, *[You may address her by her first name if that's how she introduced herself at the interview.]*

Just a note to thank you for taking the time to speak with me this afternoon about the customer service position at XYZ. The information you gave me about your company was very helpful.

I was especially impressed with the company's customer orientation. It has been my experience that putting the customer first helps to build loyalty and repeat business. I believe it's the only way to go! I was also pleased to learn about the teamwork emphasis in your office. As you know, my background includes work on a number of team projects.

I hope I was able to convey to you my enthusiasm for your company. XYZ has built a reputation as a leader in service and customer support, and I can see why. I would welcome the opportunity to become a part of your team.

Thank you again. I look forward to hearing from you.

Sincerely,

Shawn Donaldson

Shawn Donaldson

of you the next time around. You have nothing to lose with this effort, and you may benefit from it.

One final word of warning: Most interviewers bring a modicum of courtesy and proficiency to the process, but you can also expect to encounter rudeness, incompetence, and the very worst in human relations. The lack of professionalism among many hiring managers and personnel departments is appalling, even in some large and prestigious companies. You may get your hopes up for an interview, buy a new outfit, practice answering questions, give up an afternoon or a whole day, give the performance of your life, and write a wonderful thank-you note, only to leave and never hear a word, not even a polite rejection letter. (Of course, if you're really interested, you should be contacting the employer within a week or two anyway, but there's no excuse for someone in the company not following through in some way.) You may be told to wait indefinite lengths of time after the interview for an answer, you may not even be able to get an answer, you may meet with interviewers who haven't looked at your résumé or application and have no clue what to ask you, you may be asked to wait and wait for the interview once you've arrived with no explanation and no apology, or you may be asked rude, inappropriate, and even illegal questions.

One man told of rearranging a busy schedule for an interview, only to be told that the woman he was to speak to was out of town and no one there had ever heard of the applicant. A successful and attractive saleswoman told of going to an interview in which a large, cigar-smoking interviewer began by looking her all over and then asking, "What's a broad like you want to work here for?" As it turned out, she didn't.

If something similar happens to you, do not take it personally. None of this reflects on you. In recent years there has been an increase in rudeness in our culture and a marked decline in simple courtesies. Am I telling you something you haven't already observed? If people in general are less likely to be polite and courteous in social situations, it's to be expected that people in business will have similar deficiencies as well.

My advice when you encounter an interviewer whose behavior is rude or insensitive is twofold. First, remember that the interview goes two ways, and like the woman mentioned above, you have the option to decide that you do not want to work in a given environment. Second, determine whether you can tolerate the interviewer's behavior. If the breach is not too severe, give the interviewer the benefit of the doubt. We all have bad days. If he or she is repeatedly distracted with phone calls and other interruptions, you may even mention that "it sure looks like you need help around here." An empathetic and patient response may convey the message that you're the solution to someone's problems.

If the behavior is intolerable, take the high road. Under some circumstances you may feel you need to express your concerns, politely but firmly. One man who had been a human resource manager for years interviewed with a major manufacturer. His follow-up calls were met with vague responses ("We haven't made a decision yet. Call us later."). After two months had passed, someone finally told him, "If you don't get the job, you may *never* hear from us." He was shocked and responded by emphatically telling the person how unprofessional he felt their procedures were. I believe his response to their behavior was called for and not at all improper.

However, never, *never* lower yourself to someone else's level, no matter what. Resolve to be an example of professionalism, confidence, and grace under pressure in what can be a very unprofessional, insecure, and graceless world. This may very well be the modern version of "going the second mile." As the Bible says, "Let us not become weary in doing good, for at the proper time we will reap a harvest if we do not give up" (Gal. 6:9) and "Let your conversation be always full of grace, seasoned with salt, so that you may know how to answer everyone" (Col. 4:6).

Before you enter a round of interviews, remember who you are, remember *whose* you are, and above all, remember Paul's wise and gentle words to the Christians at Philippi: "Stand firm in the Lord, dear friends" (Phil. 4:1).

Indeed!

11

"Some of My Best Friends..."

Dealing with Discrimination

Not too long ago I heard a story about an accomplished young woman with a new college degree. She did some calling, sent out résumés, and within a few months was on an airplane for a two-day interview with a company in another part of the country. When she got off the plane, she was met by the hiring committee. After an awkward introduction, they told her they were sorry but there had been a mix-up and someone else had been hired for the position. They then proceeded to make arrangements for her to fly back the same day. She wondered if it had anything to do with the fact that she was black.

In recent decades, progress has been made toward eliminating discrimination in employment, but many people with firsthand experience will tell you that it has been done with only limited success. In addition, workplace bias extends well beyond the racial and gender varieties. Some of it's legal and some of it isn't (but it still happens). Therefore, if you're searching for a new job, it would be to your benefit to be aware of factors that may serve to screen you out. With a little forewarning, you may be able to avoid some discrimination pitfalls.

Age discrimination, though illegal, is widespread. Many employers don't want to pay for years of experience, or they're afraid benefits for older candidates will be more costly, which they usually are. And while it's against the law to lay off people because they get too old, and therefore too expensive, a reorganization or a corporate buyout can provide a loophole to do just that. The wisdom of this policy is questionable, and one has to wonder about the long-term effects of trading a track record of achievement and experience for a short-term cost savings. The devastation this can cause individuals and their families is immeasurable. Many of my clients have compared it to being "thrown away like an old shoe."

Some human resource managers have told me they're leery of older candidates, not because of the money, but because they've found that more mature employees tend to be set in their ways and resistant to change. And when a workplace is in the midst of radical changes, both in terms of management philosophies and new technologies, people who insist on doing things the way they've always been done can prove to be more of a liability than a benefit to a growing company.

If you sense that your age is keeping you from landing the job you want, there are a few things you can do. First, don't give a hint of your age in your résumé or any correspondence. It has nothing to do with your qualifications—or lack thereof—to do the job. Cut your work experience off somewhere between ten and twenty years (no one wants to read about everything you've ever done anyway), and don't give the dates you graduated from high school or college, either on your résumé or on a job application. That way you're more likely to make the cut past a screening of older candidates. It's a little more difficult for an employer to turn you down because of your age once you manage to get in the door for an interview.

Second, when you speak to an employer, either over the phone or in person, make every effort to convey a spirit of enthusiasm and a willingness to learn and grow. You can reinforce this message if you keep abreast of new technologies and trends, take courses, attend seminars, and continually polish your skills. Your return will be well worth the investment of time and money.

On the other extreme, some employers are biased against younger employees. I once heard a hiring executive tell an audience that he's not at all impressed with "Generation X," and he received several agreeing nods. (The Xers, in case you haven't heard, are the twenty-something progeny of the baby boom generation.)

According to the stereotype, younger candidates want to make big money and move up quickly without paying their dues, they're not altogether reliable, and they have a poor work ethic. If you've run into some brick walls and suspect that you're being turned away because you're too young, there are some things you can do to allay this image.

Make an effort to appear eager and professional, and don't hesitate to tell a potential employer that you're not afraid of hard work and that you're reliable and honest. Speak clearly, look the interviewer in the eye, and smile like you mean it. Then make sure you live up to your promises about yourself. The best way to dispel this and any other myth is to prove it wrong with your attitude and your performance on the job.

Employers and employment agencies regularly discriminate against heavy people, even though a number of recent studies indicate that obesity may be more the result of heredity than environment. If weight has been a problem for you, talk to your doctor about it, make an effort to eat more healthy foods, and embark on an exercise program. You may be able to take off some of those pounds *and* bolster your self-confidence, both of which will help you in an interview.

Employers occasionally discriminate against people who are unemployed or who have gaps in their work history. It's best to keep a job until you get another one, although for a variety of reasons that's not always possible. Some people take temporary positions so they can demonstrate they're currently employed, as well as keep a paycheck coming in.

If you've been involved in some side projects (consulting, construction, yard work, Avon, craft sales, or whatever), these activities may well fill in for a time when you considered yourself to be unemployed. Or, if you've stayed home to care for children, you might mention in a cover letter that "I made the decision five years ago to put my career aside and stay home with my children, but I'm eager to get back to the business world." A word of warning: Employers are more likely to be understanding if the person who stayed home with children is a woman. Although wage and promotion discrimination remain problems for women in all fields, this is an example of reverse discrimination.

Some employers may be hesitant to hire you if you've been self-employed because they're afraid that after working for yourself for any length of time you'll be uncomfortable taking directions from someone else. You don't always have to describe yourself as "self-employed" or "owner" on an application or a résumé. Instead, call yourself a manager or a consultant for such-

and-such a company, which is what you are, even if you own the company.

Having too many jobs in your work history may present another area of potential discrimination. Try to find ways to edit them down by combining similar jobs (i.e., School Teacher, West Elementary, Westville, Indiana, and Blackstone Elementary, Blackstone, Indiana, 1990 to 1996) or by eliminating some altogether, particularly jobs that you held for under a year. If you exclude the months and go strictly by years when giving dates of employment (which a lot of people do anyway), the gaps will be less evident.

Believe it or not, too *few* jobs can also give a prospective employer pause. It used to be that if you worked for the same company for twenty years it was a sign of stability. Today it may evoke concerns that you've been indoctrinated into another company's way of doing things and won't adapt well to a transition. Indicate on your résumé the job changes and progression you've experienced throughout your tenure with the company. Make it clear that even though you worked for one employer, you wore a number of hats and held a wide range of responsibilities. Also demonstrate any continuing education and seminars you've attended. These examples will show flexibility on your part and help to allay the concerns of a prospective employer.

You cannot possibly anticipate or avoid every prejudice, but you can take steps to dodge some of them, and that may make all the difference.

12

"So, You're a Christian . . ."

Facing Religious Discrimination

It seemed like a good idea. My credentials as a résumé writer and career consultant and my previous experience in trying to reenter the workplace after years at home made me uniquely qualified. And so I wrote to a social service agency with a history of providing support to women. I proposed a workshop for women who wanted to reenter the workforce, and I offered to waive the usual honorarium and allow all proceeds to go to the organization. I sent a copy of a newspaper article about my work and waited for the phone to ring.

It didn't take long. Within just a few days, the director called me and said she was interested and planned to run the idea by the board of directors. However, one thing concerned her.

"I have a problem with the fact that you're a Christian," she said, something she had gleaned from the article I had sent her. "Since we receive government funds, we would run the risk of losing them if you were to talk about your religious beliefs."

I was stunned. I told her my purpose was not to present a religious program. I thought that was obvious from the letter I'd written, and the reference in the article was so brief I'd all but forgotten about it. I said I didn't intend to bring up the subject, but of course, I had no way of anticipating the topics others might raise.

Our conversation would have gone swimmingly if only I had assured her I wouldn't bring up the subject, no matter what, but I would not and could not render such a promise. Of course, she and I both knew there is no other group of people she would single out for that kind of censorship. In addition, along with government funding, her organization received support from a host of area churches. It was hard to miss the inconsistency—and hypocrisy—inherent in her concerns.

She said she'd get back to me later, and within several months I received a letter from the organization explaining that it didn't have the staff to support such a venture. I felt a little bit like the person who's been told in an interview that she's too old, and then receives a letter saying she's been turned down for the position because her qualifications "don't meet the company needs at this time." It's a little hard to swallow a politely crafted explanation when the *real* reason behind the rejection has already been let out of the bag.

I have long been a believer in equality and social justice. Perhaps my greatest inspiration has been the Old Testament prophets, from Isaiah's warnings against exploiting the poor (10:1–2) to Amos's thunderings about justice flowing like a river (5:24). And the New Testament is filled with admonitions to treat people from all backgrounds with deference and respect, regardless of their status. Jesus himself set an extraordinary example by finding his place among the most despised of his day. As a result of these concerns, I spent more than ten years of my life working for civil rights, and during that time I heard endless stories about the effects of discrimination on people's lives, from small annoyances to serious threats. I find it somewhat ironic that I'm hearing these stories again . . . from Christians.

There is a growing tendency toward an antireligious and more specifically an anti-*Christian* bias and the singling out of Christians for discrimination in the workplace, as the following examples illustrate. This can be particularly threatening to those who are seeking employment.

A woman with a successful track record in insurance sales inquired about becoming an agent for a particular company. The people she spoke with at the company were delighted, and she began to go through their screening process. One of the things they required, she was told, was that she must agree never, under any circumstances, to talk about religion with any of her clients. She declined, and so did they.

A young man began attending a local church and became involved in a study group and the youth program. Somehow the subject came up in the office during the week, and he talked about some of his church activities with co-workers. He was overheard by a supervisor who pulled him aside and gave him some friendly advice: "If you want a future with this company, don't let people hear you talking about that kind of stuff."

A man who had put in overtime to complete a project for his company was told without warning that he had to work late one evening. When he said he was leading a Bible study that night, and besides, his part of the project was completed, he was criticized

for putting his church and his family above his job.
Six days later he was fired.

And so it goes. Unless you've personally encountered
them, you're probably oblivious to their existence, but
the jabs of anti-Christian bias abound, and people of
faith, with increasing frequency, are made to feel defensive. When it happened to me, my initial reaction
was to stew for a few days and then go into a full-blown
state of righteous indignation and outrage. I wanted to
call a press conference, I wanted to write to the organization's contributors and board members, I wanted to
publicly garner the support of the Christian community against it. I'm grateful now that the Lord kept me
from acting on my impulses. Time, reason, and a good
dose of supernatural grace have given me a more balanced perspective.

For starters, it helps to understand the nature of prejudice. Literally, prejudice means to "pre-judge." One
may assume that Italians have hot tempers, Irish are
shifty, African-Americans have rhythm, Arabs are ter-
rorists, women have limited reasoning abilities, or that
Christians are narrow-minded people who aren't capa-
ble of relating to the real world, and then go on to pre-
judge others based on these assumptions. At the heart
of any prejudice is ignorance, pure and simple. We form
a stereotyped image in our mind because of limited experience, poor upbringing, or media images, and we
make judgments based on inadequate understanding
and limited knowledge. Yes, hate sometimes plays a factor, but more often it's just plain ignorance. And by the
way, we Christians are fooling ourselves if we believe
we are immune from the snare of ignorance and prejudice, so we dare not be overly judgmental here.

I do not believe the way to counter ignorance is to rail
against it. In fact, I am convinced that doing so only po-

larizes people further, and we already have enough groups huddling together in their trenches, caught up furiously in a war of words. We have lost, it seems, the fine art of dialog and reason as every conceivable special interest group vies for the opportunity to air its grievances. I'm uncomfortable with the strident, in-your-face approach that has become so popular among political groups of both the left and the right these days. As a Christian, I am extremely conscious of the fact that my life is a reflection of Jesus Christ, and as a result, I strive to follow his—and not the world's—agenda in getting my point across. This means I do not have to win every battle or argument, prove every point, lambast my opponent, or pulverize the enemy. The confrontational approach does have its merits under some circumstances, but it would behoove us to remember that Jesus won his greatest victory from a twisted and ugly Roman cross.

And so I have decided not to publicly name the organization. The fact is the people in the organization are doing a lot of good, and I don't want to hinder that. But I do speak one on one with people affiliated with the organization in various capacities, and I share my concerns in the hopes of raising awareness and countering the ignorance.

I generally encourage Christians who have encountered discrimination in employment to take a similar approach. Before we become paranoid ourselves, let's look at this in perspective. It's true that the antireligious trend is alarming, and this may well lead to some more serious threats down the road. But for right now, as "persecution" goes, this is pretty mild given the fact that in some parts of this world Christians are in fear for their lives. In addition, we have an opportunity here to dispel the myth and enlighten the ignorant by demonstrating integrity, dedication, and a solid work ethic when on the job. I believe Jesus referred to this as letting our light shine.

Given all that, it's still my job to tell employment seekers that religious affiliation may best be left unmentioned until after a job offer is secure. And this is not just my advice. In his highly touted best-seller, *Knock 'em Dead: The Ultimate Job Seeker's Handbook*, Martin Yate includes a section on how to field illegal questions in a job interview. He suggests that the interviewer be given the benefit of the doubt (the question, after all, may be completely innocent), and that the best response is usually a polite and straightforward one. He then goes on to give sample replies to queries about age, marital status, and family plans. But his answer to the question "What religion do you practice?" is telling. If you do practice, he suggests that you say, "I attend my church/synagogue/mosque regularly, but I make it my practice not to involve my personal beliefs in my work. The work for the company and my career are too important for that."[4] He warns that any kind of response that doesn't indicate a total sellout to the company (my words, not his) may limit your chances of landing the all-important job offer.

Donald Asher drives home a similar point, albeit with a little more finesse, in *From College to Career: Entry-Level Résumés for Any Major*. He warns that "serving in a fundamentalist Christian community outreach organization might be important to you as a person, but for you as a candidate it could be job-search poison."[5]

This may all be very sensible advice given the uncertainty of the job market these days. But there's something at the heart of this matter that is more than a little disconcerting.

It seems to be a given that religious belief is really not all that important, or at least it shouldn't be. Or if it is, we're not supposed to tell anyone, because if word gets out, it will be . . . well, job-search poison. What's really important here, we must remember, is a career, a job, security, a future. Religion is to be stored away in a closet somewhere as we sell ourselves to the highest bidder. It was just this business of what's important and what's not that was the subject of Jesus' Sermon on the Mount. Jesus, as usual, had a very different view of things. He went beyond the generally accepted standards of moral responsibility and said that we are not only to guard our actions but our hearts as well. We are to love and pray for our enemies, abstain from even thinking about immoral behavior, and give more than is expected of us—and in secret, no less!

In Matthew 6 Jesus goes on to tell us that we are to submit our whole lives to God, and to live with complete confidence. "Do not be worried about the food and drink you need in order to stay alive, or about clothes for your body. After all, isn't life worth more than food? And isn't the body worth more than clothes?" (Matt. 6:25 GNB).

Well, isn't it? It's hard to tell amid the din and clamor for money, jobs, benefits, and security, and it's especially difficult to keep this perspective when faced with decreasing wages or unemployment and a highly competitive job market. The inevitable temptation is to do whatever it is that has to be done to get what you need. Can you work on Sundays? Sure, any time. Will your beliefs interfere with the way we do things around here? Not a chance. Are you willing to make the company your number one priority? Absolutely. What's the most important thing in your life? Whatever you want it to be.

But Jesus beckons over the call of this world, and he makes a promise. He says that if we concern ourselves above everything else with the kingdom of God and with what God requires of us, then he will provide us with all these other things (see Matt. 6:33). We will have food and clothing and shelter; we will be able to pay our bills and care for our families.

We cannot forget that we have another obligation, and we are called to a higher standard. And so I have decided that Donald Asher's advice that job applicants tone down religious affiliation is probably worth considering, and Martin Yate's suggestion that we sacrifice our souls at the corporate altar is out of the question. And I am reminded of an experience of my own, years ago, before I learned about all the clever strategies necessary to land a job.

I was on a final interview for an all-important position. The corporate president asked some general questions and then said pointedly, "What is the most important thing in your life?" I hesitated nervously and finally answered, "Well, I'm a Christian . . ."

"No, no, no," he said, waving his hand in the air as if to tell me that was the wrong answer. "I mean," he continued, "what is the *core* of your life?"

I paused for a moment, took a breath, and then replied evenly, "The core of my life is Jesus Christ."

As it turned out, I didn't get that all-important position. Today I know a whole lot more about how precarious the job market can be and how important it is to be prepared with the right answers, but I don't regret my response one bit. I hadn't given the slightest indication about my faith on my résumé, I didn't wear religious artifacts, and I avoided any uninvited religious talk, but when I was asked point blank, I knew there was only one answer. There aren't specific guidelines for every scenario, but Christians know there is a point at which we must draw the line, even in an area as critical as our career and livelihood.

Jesus said that "all men will hate you because of me" (Mark 13:13), and the apostle wrote, "Do not be surprised . . . if the world hates you" (1 John 3:13). We need to be aware of the ignorance and hostility that is directed toward us and be wise in our judgments. But we also need to say with Paul that we are not ashamed of the gospel of Jesus Christ. There will undoubtedly be a price to pay for that allegiance, but Jesus reminds us that life is a great deal more than the things we have. We belong to him, and we are not for sale to this world. God has promised that he will take care of us, and we can take him at his Word.

13

Don't Go with the Flow

Making a Difference

A woman who's worked for more than twenty years in bookkeeping and clerical positions for a growing company comes in to update her résumé. When I ask what her title is, she says matter-of-factly, "The majority of the employees in the company are clerical, and we've been told by management that we don't have titles because we just have *jobs*, not *careers*."

A man who's worked for more than ten years in inventory control and warehousing for a well-known producer tells about low pay, as well as efforts by management to discredit, malign, and get rid of longtime employees who've been injured on the job through no fault of their own. When a worker approached a manager with some valid complaints, he was dismissed with the remark, "We can replace you in a minute. You guys are a dime a dozen."

A supervisor for a public relations firm sits in a management meeting. She voices her concern about the company's reorganization, which has led to a growing disregard, even contempt, for its employees. This is an alarming trend, she says, and it's beginning to contradict some of the promises and commitments she's made to her own staff. Several in the meeting respond by laughing and telling her in an arrogant and condescending tone that she's just naive about modern American business procedures. None of her concerns are taken seriously. It has apparently not occurred to these managers that a poisoned business environment may one day turn on *them.*

An assistant manager for the branch office of a business, with full managerial responsibilities, tells of a robbery in which a clerk was threatened. After the robber left, the assistant manager moved all employees outside into the rain because of some safety concerns. When the CEO and upper management came on the scene, they talked to each other and to the press, but they never said one word—then or at a later time—to the assistant manager, the clerk, or any of the other workers. Their concern was for their company but clearly not the safety and well-being of their employees.

Perhaps you're a foreman or a shift supervisor or a project director or a manager or a CEO—or maybe you will be someday. That may be hard to imagine if you've been pounding the pavement and talking eagerly, hopefully to people who have the power to hire, but there's a chance that you'll be one of those people one day yourself. Given that, it may be a good idea to think about the kind of supervisor you want to be. Can you care about the people under you and still do your job effectively, helping your company make a profit? A lot of people these days seem to think that the two are mutually exclusive, as the examples above illustrate, but the evidence suggests otherwise.

There are a number of very promising trends in industry today. Companies are moving toward an emphasis on teamwork, the "empowerment" of employees has become a buzzword, and the philosophy of "Total Quality Management" is based on the radical notion that companies that treat their employees well, in spite of some short-term costs, will get more productivity out of those employees in the long run. Many of these ideas coincide with biblical principles.

But there are some trends that are not so good. Greater competition from international markets and radical changes in the economy have made most companies extremely cost conscious. In and of itself that's not a bad thing; in fact, it can be very good. If companies had been more cost conscious in the past, perhaps we wouldn't be facing as many of these problems. But in the rush to hold down costs and increase profit margins there has been a trend toward a utilitarian view of workers: treating employees as merely a means to an end and as people who can be discarded once they have served their purpose.

In addition to layoffs and arbitrary cutbacks, many workers are being asked to bear a greater workload, resulting in unprecedented levels of stress and burnout. According to a *Newsweek* cover story, nearly half of all American businesses have reduced their workforce since the mid-1980s, and today's organizations routinely ask one employee to do the work of 1.3 people for the same pay, with less time off. Overtime is at an all-time high, an average of 4.7 hours per week, while the average yearly vacation and other paid absences have decreased by 3.5 days.[6]

Along with increasing levels of stress among workers at all levels, trust between management and workers—as well as management and upper management—has been seriously eroded in many companies. People tell me all the time, "I just don't know how much longer I can work in that environment." One woman told me she loves her job, but the company she works for "has cancer." Workers at all levels are scared and angry, and in many cases rightfully so.

This presents a unique and unprecedented challenge to those of us who are followers of Jesus Christ, not only to trust him when we experience the pangs of discrimination or job elimination, but to use whatever influence we may have to demonstrate the love of Christ in an often cold and loveless world.

God may very well use any painful experiences you've encountered along the way to make you more sensitive to others in the future. Perhaps he will give you the opportunity to speak out against policies that discriminate, to provide support and encouragement to those who have been treated unfairly, or to take the lead in implementing policies for treating employees in a fair and equitable manner.

This is sure to cost something, but research has shown that when employers respect and empower their employees, these companies are likely to be much stronger in the long run. Back in 1981 there was a best-selling book called *In Search of Excellence* in which two management experts studied the most successful corporations in America to discover what they had in common, and what the authors found was that all those corporations treated their employees well. If you treat people well, if you respect and empower them, it stands to reason that you will build loyalty, commitment, teamwork, and productive workers. It's hard to imagine that one would have to conduct a major study to discover that.

According to the writers,

> Our findings were a pleasant surprise. The project
> showed, more clearly than could have been hoped for,
> that the excellent companies were, above all, brilliant
> on the basics. Tools didn't substitute for thinking. In-
> tellect didn't overpower wisdom. Analysis didn't impede
> action. Rather, these companies worked hard to keep
> things simple in a complex world. They persisted. They
> insisted on top quality. They fawned on their customers.
> They listened to their employees and treated them like
> adults. . . . The excellent companies treat the rank and
> file as the root source of quality and productivity gain.
> They do not foster we/they labor attitudes.[7]

We may be well into the '90s, but this is hardly outdated.
According to author and business prognosticator Roger
Herman, as many as 77 percent of employees are dissat-
isfied with their jobs, and he warns of a coming labor shortage, accompanied by an "unprecedented churning of the
labor force" as we approach the year 2000, with people
jumping from job to job like never before. As the competition heats up for competent and loyal workers, it will be
those companies notorious for their poor work environment that will lose. "The wisest thing a company can do,"
intones Herman, "is hang onto the people they have."[8]

It never ceases to amaze me how true God's promises
are—and how slow we can be to grasp that fact. We are
to follow biblical principles because they are right and
fair, but in the end there is a bonus: They pay off! The
fact is people who go against the flow and decide to move
into the twenty-first century *without* losing sight of those
who work for them will have a healthier, stronger workforce. And that is a decidedly enviable resource in these
changing times.

14

Slings and Arrows

Surviving the Tough Times

"How weary, stale, flat and unprofitable seem to me all the uses of this world," said Hamlet in the play of the same name penned by William Shakespeare.

Hamlet was, I think it's safe to say, clinically depressed. His father's death was followed rapidly by his mother's remarriage. The prince was facing what seemed to him the loss of *both* parents, and it was as if he'd lost his own place in the world as well. He grieved and agonized over the "slings and arrows of outrageous fortune," he festered with bitterness, he feared God, and he was angry with God. This young man found no peace and no purpose in life, and ultimately his struggles led to his demise. His story has resonated throughout four centuries as a classic tragedy.

Hamlet would have felt quite at home, I think, in the late twentieth century. In an international study of mood disorders, researchers at Cornell University concluded that "among generations reaching maturity after 1945, depression seems to be on the rise and occurs at a younger age."[9] We are, it would seem, a planet filled with people who, like Hamlet, possess an increasingly fragile sense of their place in this world. Any misfortune can trigger feelings of powerlessness, leading to the downward spiral toward depression. It's how you deal with it all that matters.

I am not a psychologist, but I talk every week to people who are experiencing unemployment, downsizing, career elimination, and job loss, and I have made some observations. First, it's essential in the midst of a personal crisis to develop a plan of action and to carry out that plan. That's why I stress developing personal inventories, creating a script, and making a set number of calls a day. All of this results in a sense of power and control that is essential for personal well-being. (And besides, it works!)

In addition to carrying out an action plan, I have observed that without exception those who weather the transition with the least amount of depression and debilitating discouragement are people who are focused outside of themselves.

A client came into my office after three months of trying to find a job. He'd had absolutely no success, and he was beginning to feel as if his life were over. We talked at length about his skills and how he might focus his job search, and I helped him devise a more aggressive strategy for using his new résumé. Finally, he said to me, "I feel so useless. I have always had somewhere to go and something to do when I got up in the morning. Now when I talk to people, I don't know what to say. I feel as if I'm not even a person anymore."

These are common feelings for someone going through a job loss, and I suggested that he consider volunteering some of his time, even a few hours a week, at one of the many area agencies. I even recommended some places where I knew his talents would be useful. "It will help you to keep your skills fresh," I told him. "You might make some good contacts, and it will give you an opportunity to use some of that free time for a good cause."

He was incredulous. "You mean work for *nothing?*" he asked me. He made it clear that was out of the question. Throughout the following year that it took him to find a job, I spoke to him many times, and each time he was still depressed.

At about the same time another client came in to see me. He had also been job searching for several months, with no results. He had a history in construction work, but an injury had virtually ended his construction career, and he had a wife and children who relied on his income. We pored over his work history and job skills together in an attempt to find suitable options, and I was struck with how positive and upbeat he was throughout the whole process. He admitted he had some extra free time on his hands, but he was helping with several activities in his church, he and his wife were providing leadership to a small couples group, and he was also performing a variety of small jobs to make ends meet. He was certain, he told me, that something would come up sooner or later, and in the meantime, they'd get by. Several months afterward I spoke with him again. He was still unemployed, and they were still struggling but managing, he told me. His attitude remained positive and confident.

The difference, of course, had nothing to do with the skills, options, successes, or failures of either candidate, but with their viewpoints. One, like our friend Hamlet, was concerned primarily with himself. The other was concerned with his own situation, of course, but he was not obsessed with it. Instead, he filled his mind, and his days, with concern for others as well. He saw his own personal dilemma in the context of a broader perspective, and that perspective kept him positive and focused.

These men stand out in sharp contrast, demonstrating two very different ways people approach stress: from a self-centered point of view versus an others-centered point of view. I have decided that the latter is by far the

better, and so I encourage people who are struggling with
a job search to resist the trap of self-absorption, which
is a sure setup for depression. Find a place where you
can make a difference, and get involved!

For a Christian, I believe the biblical call is pretty clear:
The first place for involvement is your church, the local
branch of the body of Christ that you have chosen to
make as your home. Perhaps you already *are* involved
in your church, but if you're not, I would encourage you
to take some steps in that direction.

We have become a consumer oriented culture in recent years, which is a good thing. Companies have to
work harder to compete, and the result is often a greater
emphasis on value, quality, variety, and service. But that
consumer orientation has extended to the way people
think about their church, which is not at all a good thing.
You've heard the laundry lists:

> "I'm looking for a church with a good youth program,
> and not just for teenagers. I want a program for my
> fourth grader as well."
> "I enjoy a good music program, and if a church doesn't
> have the music I love, I'll go somewhere else."
> "I want an early service so my family and I can do
> something in the afternoon."
> "I need a later service, because I hate to get up and
> rush around on Sunday morning."
> "I want a church located on the north side so that I
> won't have to go through any bad neighborhoods to
> get there."

It has become quite common for churches to pander to
this consumer mentality, adding this program and that in
order to meet the ever increasing consumer demands.

But did you notice something about those requests?
They all begin with "I." And that's the problem with the consumer mindset when applied to church. There is no sense

of the service or support that I may render, only what the church can do for *me*. In fact, I don't think I've ever heard people say they selected a church because of some talents they had that might benefit the church. ("They have a struggling music program, and I've built music programs in the past. We chose that church so I could lend them a hand in that area." Or, "Their preschool department was so disorganized. They just didn't have anyone to take charge and make it work. I saw that as an area where I could make a difference.") We are called, after all, to the example of Jesus Christ, who came to this earth to serve. I fear that the emphasis on what I can *get* over and above what I can *give* may lead to increasing numbers of immature and self-centered Christians.

So if by chance you find that you are exceedingly comfortable in your church, or if you're in the market for a church that will make you feel that way, perhaps you should rethink things. Get out of yourself, look around, and see what you can do. Does a Sunday school room need painting? Is the church in need of a youth director? Is the education program lacking a teacher? Ask God to help you find a place in his church and in your community, where you might use the talents he gave you. Offer yourself in service, and you'll find that all the problems that loomed so large in your mind will somehow grow smaller and more manageable. Your involvement will help you keep your confidence and energy levels high—invaluable assets when searching for a job!

As if the things I've said aren't controversial enough, I'm going to go a step further—right over the edge. There's one more thing I recommend—tithe.

Tithe? Have you lost your mind? Our income has been cut in half in the past year and then we had those hospital bills and the car broke down and the washer had to be overhauled . . .

Yes, *tithe,* sometimes called "the T word," which means to give 10 percent of your income. Actually, asking people to tithe in the midst of a crisis does seem a little extreme, especially since studies have indicated that most Christians don't even tithe when things are going well. But I am a firm believer in tithing, not because of what it does for the recipient, but because of what it does for the giver.

Tithing is a bold and confident way of saying that we believe in the providence and faithfulness of God, and in the most quoted tithing passage in the Bible, God goes so far as to dare us to tithe.

"'Will a man rob God? Yet you rob me. . . . You are under a curse—the whole nation of you—because you are robbing me. Bring the whole tithe into the storehouse . . . Test me in this,' says the LORD Almighty, 'and see if I will not throw open the floodgates of heaven and pour out so much blessing that you will not have room enough for it'" (Mal. 3:8–11).

If, like so many, you are struggling to balance a declining income with increasing costs, the prospect of tithing may seem overwhelming, outrageous, terrifying. But in fact, tithing is a joy! I am continually amazed that when we put God first and give him his tenth off the top (not from what's left over), everything else falls into place. I have seen many new Christians tithe, timidly and with trepidation at first, only to shake their heads in astonishment when somehow the bills always get paid, and God is remarkably faithful and true to his Word. It all comes down to Jesus' promise in the Sermon on the Mount that if we seek first God's righteousness and God's kingdom, all of these other things will be given to us as well (see Matt. 6:33). What we are really saying when we fail to tithe is that we don't trust God with our resources. In this day when people are so beset by fears about money and security, I believe that the decision to tithe is one of the most important we can make.

Depression, of course, can have a mind of its own in spite of our best efforts. If you continue to struggle with bouts of despondency, or the feeling that you're free-falling into an abyss, you may consider joining or even starting a support group for people who are job hunting. These organizations have become common in recent years, and many people have said that being part of a group helps them to feel more connected and less isolated. These groups allow people to share job search strategies, swap information about jobs and companies, and encourage one another through the ups and downs of what can be a long and lonely time of career transition.

It helps to remember that being a Christian does not make one immune to hardship by any means, but it does give us resources that others don't have. Sometimes they kick in automatically, as when we encounter tragedy or uncertainty and are enveloped with an inexplicable sense of peace. More often they require a response or an action on our part. If you take the passive approach to sustaining your faith, you are likly to find it waning.

If the kingdom is first, both in our time and our money, then we are not likely to be prey to "the slings and arrows of outrageous fortune" as are others around us. There is no place for a sense of purposelessness. Like lights in the darkness, we are called to live lives of confidence and joy, marked by humble service to our God.

15

Recession-Proof Your Job Skills

Planning for the Future

No matter how desperate you may feel, don't rush to accept an offer if it's not what you want. Accepting a job offer is a little bit like getting married. Once you take the plunge, you determine your course for many years, possibly the rest of your life. If you decide you don't like the position, or the company, you can either bail out or hang in there, but neither is good for your long-term career—or your emotional well-being. Consider any offer very carefully, and make sure it's what you want before you say yes.

Since raises are based on current earnings, the salary you accept will determine your salary for the rest of your history with the company. If you accept something that is five thousand dollars below what you should receive, you'll be five thousand dollars or more behind in raises, promotions, and bonuses for your entire tenure with an organization. If you receive an offer that interests you, don't be afraid to negotiate a little. A company invests a lot of time and money in selecting a candidate.

They don't want to lose you now, so you have some leverage at this point that you will probably never have again.

Once you have landed the job you want, your goal is to become as invaluable to your employer as you possibly can. But you also want to stay up-to-date so that you'll be ready should you need to embark on another job search down the road, and the odds are that you will. Experts recommend you keep in mind three things if you are going to attain any kind of job security in today's changing work climate: teamwork, continuing education, and flexibility.

1. Teamwork. The old days of the "Lone Ranger" worker are gone. As the amount of information increases beyond the ability of any one person to keep up with it all, workers will need to learn to operate effectively in a teamwork environment. As a worker or a supervisor, you'll need to be able to foster teamwork among people at all levels, become cross trained in various positions, and move away from the old notion of independent employees working in isolation from one another.

2. Continuing education. A growing number of new jobs require the ability to acquire and apply ever changing technical knowledge. Continuous learning is key. If you haven't completed a formal education—and this may range, depending on your field, from vocational training or an associate's degree to a master's degree or higher—this is something you may want to look into. If you're young (in your twenties to early or midthirties—and the younger and more inexperienced you are, the more important this is), I recommend you give some thought to pursuing formal education of some kind. As the competition heats up for the better jobs, the people with the degrees are going to have the advantages.

I realize that going to school while trying to pay the bills can be frustrating, and it can take what seems like forever, but completing your education may be more important than ever. The secretary of labor has said that today there is a higher correlation between education, earnings, and benefits than in any time in the history of our country.[10] So hang in there and don't get discouraged! In ten years you will still be competing for jobs, and you will either have that degree or you won't. If you have it, believe me, you will be very glad you do.

If you're older and have a solid base of experience, a degree may not be worth the time and trouble it will cost you. At this point your experience may well be worth its weight in gold, and then some. I've seen people put successful careers and sometimes even their families on hold to complete a degree program, only to find that the degree failed to give them all the new options they had hoped it would.

Regardless of whether you pursue a degree, you need to keep pace with the trends in your field. In order to keep up, you will need to read and attend seminars on a regular basis. In addition to job-related training, you need to continually develop your problem-solving and communication skills.

Problem solving may be the most important skill you'll take to the workplace, because employers are looking above all for people who can solve problems. In order to be an effective problem solver, you need critical-thinking skills. This goes far beyond just memorizing the correct answers or steps one, two, and three in performing a job. It means that you listen, observe, ask questions, and think creatively about the situations that you encounter in life and on the job. And believe it or not, considering the subtleties in a work of great literature, or the factors that led to the Second World War, or the implications of the laws of thermodynamics are all disciplines that help develop critical-thinking and problem-solving skills. So add some mental gymnastics to your life. Regularly study and read, and don't just choose books and articles that are easy for you; read things that require you to stretch your thinking abilities. Explore, think great thoughts, ask hard questions, and keep mentally active.

In addition, communication skills are listed by many employers as one of the most desirable traits. Remember, teamwork is the magic word for the twenty-first century. If you are going to work as a part of a team, you will have to be able to cooperate and collaborate with co-workers, subordinates, supervisors, customers, and just about everyone else. If you lack social skills, if you're ignorant about simple courtesies, if you cannot explain what you're doing or write a report, you have a serious handicap. Reading and staying mentally alert will help, but if you're weak when it comes to communicating, you may want to consider taking a course on public speaking or business writing.

3. Flexibility. Finally, if you find yourself saying, "Why are we doing it this way now? We did it the old way for years and never had any problems" or "Why do I have to learn this? I can't see how this is necessary"—bite off your tongue! Peter Drucker, writing for *The Atlantic Monthly*, has said that "No century in recorded history has experienced so many social transformations and such radical ones as the twentieth century."[11] The workforce is in the midst of overwhelming social and technological upheaval, and this climate of change will only accelerate. Only the workers who adapt will be able to keep up.

I have a confession on this count. I preach the importance of keeping up with changing technology, but I have to admit I have been known to drag my feet a time or two on my way toward the twenty-first century. A bolt of lightning took out my old computer, and I was forced (some may say kicking and screaming) to upgrade to one with a lot more bells and whistles. I performed the installation myself, calling the hot lines only a dozen or more times.

I even hooked into the internet, and I'm surfing my way through books and trials and errors to understand all the ins and outs. It seems every time I conquer something new, there are ten more things I have to learn. I keep hoping that someone will come along and explain all this stuff to me, or just take care of it all so I don't have to, but so far no one has.

And that's the point. Keeping up—even if you hate to do it and have all the technical aptitude of a fence post— is essential, and the initiative to do so has to come from *you.* Like anything else, taking the initiative will give you a sense of control and confidence that will make your life more challenging and meaningful, even as it gives you more options for the future.

Don't lose sight of the fact that you are going to spend a large percentage of your life at your job. Deciding what to do, getting the training necessary to do it, and adapting to changes so that you can do it well are all part of an investment that will pay off in a big way down the road. If you set your mind to it, there's a good chance you can make the "workquake" work for you!

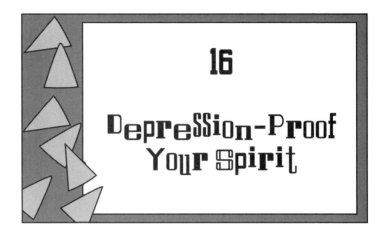

16

Depression-Proof Your Spirit

Looking to the Future

The positive and creative approach is critically important, but in the end there are limits to just how much we can control. The economy will move in directions that no one can predict or manage, and in spite of our best efforts, we may find the foundations beneath our feet crumbling. That is why, in the midst of the upheaval going on around us, we need to make sure our roots are grounded deeply in Christ. As the apostle Paul admonished Christians at Colosse, "So then, just as you received Christ Jesus as Lord, continue to live in him, rooted and built up in him, strengthened in the faith as you were taught, and overflowing with thankfulness" (Col. 2:6–7).

As a former teacher, I don't put much stock in cramming at the last minute. I've seen students come in for tests with bloodshot eyes, hunched backs, and dragging feet. One once said to me, "I stayed up all night and studied. I feel like I'm in a coma." Not a great way to ace an exam, wouldn't you agree? Students who have kept up during the semester are far more apt to be ready for the big exam, both physically and mentally.

It's the same thing with the Christian walk. If we are to be rooted and built up in Christ, solid enough in the faith to withstand the assaults of the world and the enemy, then we cannot count on cramming at the last minute; we will need to do the advance work. Support your church with your time and your money, attend church regularly, read and study your Bible, both on your own and in a Bible study of some kind, and make prayer a priority in your life. These are the commitments that make for mature and strong faith. As the Lord said through the prophet Isaiah, "If you do not stand firm in your faith, you will not stand at all" (Isa. 7:9). But the converse of that is true as well. For when the world's foundations fall apart, those who have kept the faith will surely be found standing.

Often we respond to stress or loss with a sense of shock, as if that's not supposed to happen to us. Where did we ever get that idea? There are no promises that we won't have to struggle in this life. In fact, Jesus tells us, "In this world you will have trouble." The key is not whether or not we'll encounter difficulties, but where our priorities will be when we do. If our hearts and our lives are anchored in Jesus Christ, we will be ready. "Take heart!" Jesus told his disciples. After all, "I have overcome the world" (see John 16:33).

As you embark on the adventure of a job search, and throughout the ups and downs of life that you will surely encounter, that is a promise to remember!

Appendix

How to Choose a Résumé Service

While you're looking for a job, you're in sales, and the marketing brochure you use to sell yourself is your résumé. A good résumé won't get you a job, but it may get you an interview. If you've read the books about how to write a résumé and you've made the effort but you just aren't happy with what you're coming up with, you may decide it's time to call a résumé writing service. This type of service offers you the opportunity to work with someone who will be more objective in drawing out your history and skills and who has more experience—and possibly some training—writing résumés. But there are several listed in the phone book. How do you know which one to call?

First, it helps to know that anyone can hang out a sign and call himself or herself a résumé writer, so you need to shop around, and although cost is an important factor, it should by no means be your primary consideration. You are not calling hardware stores to get the cheapest price on a power drill. All résumé services are *not* created equal.

Résumé services vary widely in what they offer. Many are straight typing services: You bring in a draft of what you want and someone types it for you. Some services offer written guidelines to help you write your own résumé. Others employ people who will make minor changes (mostly grammar and spelling) on your work. If you go with this kind of service, ask if they offer upgrades as your career progresses, how long they've been in business, and the type of equipment they use. Laser printing is the highest quality, and if you're paying to have someone else typeset your résumé, I wouldn't settle for anything less.

The advantage of this kind of service is that it is less expensive than professional writing services. If you know exactly what you want on your résumé and aren't interested in input from an objective party, this is the way to go.

At some services you fill out a form, something like a job application, and someone prepares the résumé from the information you've given, with little or no individual consultation. This requires some writing and layout so the price will be somewhat higher, but again, you're dealing primarily with a typing service.

Services that emphasize *writing* usually do the layout and printing, and may provide a form for you to fill out, but a consultant also spends a fair amount of time with a client before preparing a draft, as well as after it's completed to make revisions. This can be done in person or over the phone and via the mail. The advantage of this kind of service is that you are working with an objective person, and if that person is good at the job, he or she will be able to pull things out of you that you never thought of putting on a résumé, sift out irrelevant information, and help you focus your résumé to achieve the highest impact. A consultant should also be up-to-date with the latest résumé styles and formats. If this is what you want, make sure you're speaking to a writer, not just a receptionist, when you call to inquire about an organization's services, and don't be afraid to ask for credentials. What is the educational background of the writers? This isn't the most important consideration, but a degree in journalism, English, communication, marketing, or business may be a plus.

Also ask about any professional writing or business experience, aside from résumé writing, that the writers have done, how many years experience they have writing résumés, and how much time they generally spend with a client before preparing a personalized résumé.

Ask about membership in the Professional Association of Résumé Writers (PARW), which includes a subscription to a journal with up-to-date information and book reviews in the field of résumé writing and career consulting. You may even ask about continuing education. Have they attended any PARW conventions? If you go to their office, look for books on résumé writing, interviewing, job hunting, and the like.

Ask if the service has a Certified Professional Résumé Writer (CPRW) on staff. The certification is conferred by PARW and requires passing a comprehensive four-part test, as well as submitting samples of work to a nationwide panel of experts in the field. In addition, the certification is recognized by the *Guide to National Certification Programs* published annually by the Human Resource Development Press. If a writer is certified, it's a sure sign you're working with someone who has met some objective standards as a résumé consultant.

Ask not only *what* a service charges but *how* it charges. It's to be expected that a résumé for a biochemist with a

Ph.D. and twenty years of experience will cost more than a résumé for a high school graduate with three years experience working at a grocery store. Some writers charge strictly by the hour and can usually give you an estimate before they begin to work. Others use various criteria, such as style, length, number of years experience, and the career track of the applicant to determine cost. If you talk to a service that charges one flat fee for just about everyone, it's a good indication that your résumé will be standardized.

Ask about updating services (usually there's a charge but at a reduced rate), and also ask how long the company has been in business. If you think you'll need future updating (and most people do), you want to make sure the company will be there when you come back. A business that has just gotten started may not be your best bet.

Also listen. Does the consultant ask you any questions, or just quote prices? Does he or she indicate a personal interest in you? You may ask if he or she does many résumés in your field, and don't just take yes for an answer. Listen carefully to see if the consultant sounds knowledgeable in your particular field, or if he or she asks you questions relevant to your line of work. A good résumé service acts in collaboration with clients, and that collaboration usually begins with the first phone call. When someone calls me he or she invariably wants to know the cost, and I can't possibly give even a ballpark figure unless I know something of the person's history and the kind of job he or she will be looking for. So I begin by asking questions and perhaps even making suggestions about how to focus the résumé and where there might be openings in his or her field. The consultation often begins before the first appointment.

Once you have decided on a résumé service, there are some things you can do to help your résumé writer get the most out of the initial consultation. There are two kinds of clients who make my job more difficult: those who talk too much and those who talk too little. A résumé consultation can be an invigorating experience. A résumé writer's job is to emphasize the positive, and it can be a real ego boost. There's nothing wrong with that; confidence is important to an effective job search, and lots of people in the job market *need* an ego boost. But some people are so encouraged by the consultation process that they take it as an invitation to go off on tangents that are unrelated to the task at hand.

To some extent that's to be expected. I try to create a relaxed and open rapport with my clients, and in the course of a conversation it's natural for them to give me more details on a particular situation than I need for a résumé. Often that gets the communication lines open. But sometimes I have clients who respond to every question with endless details about office politics, personal problems, life history, or unrelated interests. The result is that we have less time to talk about the things that really matter, and it may reduce the quality of the final product.

On the other hand, there are clients who come in, fill out a form, and hand it to me with one-or two-word answers to every question. They think that because I write résumés for a living I should be able to crank out their particular history without any input from them.

Wrong! Although a good résumé writer will know what questions to ask, everyone is unique, and a résumé should convey that uniqueness. The purpose of the consultation is to ferret out the special skills and accomplishments of an individual, but if the individual won't talk, then that task is hampered. If you're not much of a conversationalist, I recommend you give this some thought *before* you go in for the interview. Build an inventory list of your goals, skills, and accomplishments ahead of time, and be ready to discuss them.

When your résumé is completed, make sure you will have ample time to review everything. This is usually done in the office, but if you prefer to take it home for a day or two, a good consultant will encourage that. Check everything very carefully, including the details (name, address, zip code, telephone numbers, and dates), as well as the writing and organization. If you don't feel comfortable checking it on your own, have someone you trust look it over for you, although if you show it to too many people, you're likely to get an array of conflicting advice. Be prepared to use your own judgment in collaboration with your résumé writer in making final changes.

If you have things that you want to change, be as specific as possible, and insist that you check the final copy with the changes before your copies are run. While many résumé writers are highly competent, I haven't met one yet who claimed perfection, so you need to take some responsibility for the final proofing. If you find a mistake or something you want to change after you've approved everything and your copies have been run, you'll probably have to pay for extra copies, so don't rush through this final and very important stage.

Finding a résumé writing service is a little bit like finding the right fit. By all means shop around, but be an informed shopper. Ask questions, and make your decision based on what you need, what a service has to offer, and how comfortable you feel about the person who will be doing the work. There are a number of excellent services out there, and you may very well find yourself embarking on a positive and rewarding professional relationship.

If you're interested in Career*Pro,* we do résumés for people throughout the country, and our prices start at about seventy-five dollars. You can contact us at 6738 N. Frostwood Parkway, Peoria, Illinois 61615, or call (309) 691-2445.

Notes

Introduction

1. Richard Nelson Bolles, *What Color Is Your Parachute?* (San Francisco: Ten Speed Press, 1993), 2.

2. Harvey Mackay, *Sharkproof* (New York: Harper Business, 1993), 5.

Chapter 3: A Portrait in Words

3. William Strunk Jr., and E. B. White, *The Elements of Style*, 3d ed. (New York: Macmillan, 1979), 23.

Chapter 12: "So, You're a Christian . . ."

4. Martin Yate, *Knock 'em Dead: The Ultimate Job Seeker's Handbook* (Holbrook, Mass.: Bob Adams, 1994), 183.

5. Donald Asher, *From College to Career: Entry-Level Résumés for Any Major* (Berkeley: Ten Speed Press, 1992), 67.

Chapter 13: Don't Go with the Flow

6. "Breaking Point," *Newsweek*, 6 March 1995, 56–62.

7. Thomas J. Peters and Robert H. Waterman Jr., *In Search of Excellence* (New York: Harper & Row, 1981), 13–14.

8. Lornet Turnbull, "Coming Labor Shortage Poses Grim Challenge," Knight-Ridder, *Peoria Journal Star,* 2 May 1995, sec. A5.

Chapter 14: Slings and Arrows

9. Kristin Leutwyler, "Depression's Double Standard," *Scientific American* 272, no. 6 (June 1995): 23.

Chapter 15: Recession-Proof Your Job Skills

10. Nancy Gibbs, "Working Harder, Getting Nowhere," *Time*, 3 July 1995, 19.

11. Peter F. Drucker, "The Age of Social Transformation," *The Atlantic Monthly* 274, no. 5 (November 1994): 53.

Recommended Reading

General Job Search Information

What Color Is Your Parachute? by Richard Nelson Bolles, Ten Speed Press. This book first came out in 1970, and it has been updated every year since. It's considered the bible for job seekers, and it's easy to understand why. Written with wit and wisdom, it covers everything, including job hunting techniques, avoiding depression, relocating, and interviewing. And for those who aren't quite sure what they want to be when they grow up, it has a large section on identifying skills and interests and finding a compatible career. Of particular interest is the fact that Bolles is a Christian, and although the book isn't written specifically to a Christian audience, he makes no bones about his faith. He has a wonderful chapter in the epilogue titled "How to Find Your Mission in Life."

The Overnight Job Change Strategy by Donald Asher, Ten Speed Press, 1993. This is a book designed for the highly motivated job seeker. It's chock full of suggestions for developing and pursuing leads, selling yourself at the interview, tracking your job search, and negotiating the deal once you've landed an offer. I've recommended it to a number of clients, and those who've used it have found it helpful. Not for the faint of heart! His strategies are very aggressive, but indications are they work.

Getting, Keeping, and Growing in Your Job by Bill Corbin and Kim Corbin, Beckett-Highland Publishing, 1994. Written with a rare blend of frankness and humor, this book is readable, concise, and hard-hitting. It covers applications and résumés, office politics, appearance, honesty, business ethics, and a host of other career related subjects, and it carefully avoids the manipulative job search techniques recommended by other books of this nature. As a former high school teacher, I was particularly impressed with the book's appeal to young people. But it's good for people of all ages, and you can finish it in an afternoon. As a primer for young people, it is simply the best.

Recommended Reading

National Business Employment Weekly, published weekly (as the name implies) by the *Wall Street Journal*. You can probably pick it up at your local newsstand, or you can subscribe to it by calling 1-800-JOB-HUNT. It costs about four dollars a week, and I believe it's well worth it. Although it's geared to the executive level, it has a range of articles on such topics as job hunting through the internet, interviewing, résumé writing, networking, current employment trends, and other subjects that are of benefit to just about anyone. It also includes hundreds of employment listings weekly.

Résumés and Cover Letters

Many people make the mistake of buying only one book on writing résumés and then believing whatever that book says to be engraved in stone. That's hardly the case. You would not believe how résumé books differ—and how awful some of them are. The only way to get a balanced understanding of résumé writing is to read two or more books on the subject, and then take the ideas you like from each one. I've read a number of them, and following are the ones I consider the best:

> *The Overnight Résumé* and *From College to Career: Entry-Level Résumés for Any Major* by Donald Asher, published by Ten Speed Press, 1991 and 1992 respectively, are my favorites. In what is the most practical, readable, and down-to-earth approach to writing résumés I've ever read, Asher covers everything from good writing to effective layout to all kinds of creative ways to get your message across. If you're struggling with cover letters (and when it comes to writing a cover letter, who isn't?), his book *The Overnight Job Change Letter,* Ten Speed Press, 1994, is unbeatable.
>
> *The Edge Résumé & Job Search Strategy* by Bill Corbin and Shelbi Wright, Beckett-Highland Publishing, 1993. One of the most pervasive myths about résumés is that they should sound and appear stodgy and pretentious. Baloney! Professional yes, but stuffy? Never! Your résumé is competing against hundreds if not thousands of others, and there's nothing wrong with employing some creative touches to make it stand out. This book is chock full of them, from a cover letter with a puzzle piece missing that reads "If there's

a piece missing from your organizational puzzle, I believe my background and skills will fit perfectly with your needs" (the puzzle piece shows up on the résumé) to a résumé designed as a graph to résumés with computers, money, or quotes imprinted on them, and even one for a teacher with an apple on it. This book has become a huge hit with résumé professionals nationwide, and it's easy to see why. If your job search has hit a logjam and you need some creative ideas to get it going again, this is just the book for you.

Interviewing

Sweaty Palms: The Neglected Art of Being Interviewed by H. Anthony Medley, Ten Speed Press, 1992. This book covers everything you need to know about preparing for an interview, and it will help you resist the temptation to give programmed answers to every conceivable question. It gives specific suggestions on how to tactfully and effectively gain some control of the interview, how to prepare, what to wear, how to deal with stress, how to respond to different interviewing techniques, and how to negotiate for salary and benefits. The book also includes a discussion on the importance of enthusiasm ("the exhibition of fervent interest"), and a very informative chapter about discrimination, what's legal, and what's not. The only flaw is the author's disdain for the thank-you letter. He says managers are too busy to read them and find them to be an annoyance. Wrong! I've talked to hundreds of hiring managers and every one has told me the thank-you note impresses them. Overall, this book is a great resource for building some interviewing savvy.

Anti-Christian Bias

Yes, it's real; I didn't make it up. Two books that approach from very different perspectives the topic of the growing prejudice against religious people in this country are *The Culture of Disbelief: How American Law and Politics Trivialize Religious Devotion* by Stephen L. Carter, Basic Books, 1993, and *Religious Apartheid: The Separation of Religion From American Public Life* by John Whitehead, Moody Press, 1994. Both are attorneys—Carter is a professor at Yale Law School, Whitehead is president of the Rutherford Institute—and both profess to be Christians, though Carter comes from a more liberal viewpoint, and Whitehead from a conservative bent.

Carter has some good material about anti-religious prejudice masquerading as "neutrality," the religious overtones that were characteristic of the civil rights movement of the fifties and sixties (with an interesting focus on Martin Luther King Jr. and the way he openly incorporated his faith into his efforts), the importance of religious influence in society, and a thoughtful case for vouchers for school funding. Whitehead speaks more to the question of shifting values, the inconsistencies regarding censorship, and the growing power of the state. If you want to get a feel for the very ominous trend designed to set people of faith apart from the mainstream, both of these books offer a good place to start.

In addition, *Hollywood Vs. America: Popular Culture and the War on Traditional Values,* HarperCollins/Zondervan, 1992, by Michael Medved, who is a movie reviewer and, interestingly, a practicing Jew, offers a penetrating look at the media's attack on traditional values and, specifically, Christian beliefs, reinforcing the culture's anti-Christian bias.

Related Issues

America: What Went Wrong? by Donald L. Bartlett and James B. Steele, published by Andrews and McMeel, a Universal Press Syndicate Company, 1992. This well-researched book is based on a series of articles that ran in the *Philadelphia Inquirer,* and it details with exacting precision a number of deals that led to plant closings and corporate bankruptcies, as well as numerous congressional rules, regulations, and deregulations that have resulted in fewer jobs and lower pay for a growing number of Americans. Bartlett and Steele are Pulitzer Prize-winning reporters, and their book is completely unbiased; it lambasts both the left and the right with equal fervor. If you're interested in some of the factors that led to our current state of affairs (and maybe even your unemployment), this is the book to read.

In Search of Excellence: Lessons from America's Best-Run Companies by Thomas J. Peters and Robert H. Waterman Jr., Harper & Row, 1981. This is a study of excellent companies and the philosophies and policies that made them that way.